Lydie Breeze

Lydie Breeze

PART I:
BULFINCH'S MYTHOLOGY

PART II:
THE SACREDNESS OF
THE NEXT TASK

John Guare

THE OVERLOOK PRESS
WOODSTOCK & NEW YORK

First published in the United States in 2001 by
The Overlook Press, Peter Mayer Publishers, Inc.
Woodstock & New York

WOODSTOCK:
One Overlook Drive
Woodstock, NY 12498
www.overlookpress.com
[for individual orders, bulk and special sales, contact our Woodstock office]

NEW YORK:
141 Wooster Street
New York, NY 10012

Library of Congress Cataloging-in-Publication Data

Guare, John.
Lydie Breeze / John Guare.
p. cm.
1. Nantucket Island (Mass.)—Drama. 2. Communal living—Drama. I. Title.
PS3557.U2 L9 2001   812'.54—dc21   2001021094

Book design and type formatting by Bernard Schleifer
Manufactured in the United States of America
FIRST EDITION
1 3 5 7 9 8 6 4 2
ISBN 1-58567-158-4 (PBK)
ISBN 0-7394-1929-3 (HC)

As always,
for Adele

Introduction

I ONCE SAW MY FATHER TRY TO KILL SOMEONE. YOU HAVE TO KNOW AT the top that Eddie Guare was a kind man, a sweet man, so the event of that hot summer day at the beach in 1949—when I was eleven—was all the more mysterious. (Or was it 1948, when I was ten?)

My father, who worked at the New York Stock Exchange, heard at a Christmas party on Christmas Eve in 1929 that a certain Mr. Austin had gone bankrupt in the recent disasters and would be auctioning off ocean-front property he owned on a barrier island on the South Shore of Long Island two days later.

My father got himself out to the beach and bought two prime ocean-front lots with what and for how much I don't know. He then convinced eight of his drinking buddies who had been in the First World War, the Great War, and now all worked on Wall Street to go in on this project together and build a club house for them to—well, keep the comradeship, the memory of the Great War alive. They were all on the brink of certain success. And also drink.

They were still young. Well, early to mid-30s. The future still held promise for them. And they needed a club to celebrate that. They found a three story pre-fab house in a catalogue and hired people to assemble the pieces in the kit into a club house in time for the gala summer of 1930. They called it The Dunes Club.

And now it was 1949. (Or could it have been 1950?) For nearly twenty (or exactly twenty) years, these men had been coming to this house on this beach with their girlfriends, sometimes even their wives, to drink, play cards, drink, play ping-pong, darts, drink, play horseshoes, drink, play ball, fish, bring their girls but never get trapped, and then drink. My father married his girlfriend. I was born in 1938, the only child produced after

The Dunes Club began. It was me, growing up every summer alone with these fantastic adults.

I loved going to sleep at night upstairs hearing the men and their girls below singing old songs as they washed the dishes and then played poker or bridge or sometimes horse races. They'd mark out a course on the living-room floor and bring up wooden horses from the basement. The ladies would sit on the horses. The men took turns throwing large dice on the floor, and the next horse carrying the girl of the week would advance. Hilarity! During the Second World War years, there was an unspoken bitterness. The men were too old to enlist.

Some of the men were already married, Harry married Ruthie, but Harry's German mother was a member of the Bund in Yorkville and had her photograph in the *Daily News* marching for Hitler. Ruthie was Jewish, and Harry's mother never spoke to him again. Ray had married his secretary, Eva, and his first wife wouldn't let Ray ever see his kids again. The girlfriends were introduced to me as "Lady" so when a wife might show up and question me as Elsie did—"Who was Wally here with last week?"—I couldn't say "Laura." I could only tell the truth and say "Lady. Wally was here with Lady." "But what was lady's name?" Elsie was trying to get the goods on Wally and get a divorce. But "Lady" was all I could say. I loved being part of such adult machinations.

I loved the laughter of these guys. My father's best friend, Danny, and Eddie and I would come in from a swim and take a cold water shower to wash off the salt. Danny would stand naked under the spray, his face in the water, and sing in this big operatic voice: "Figaro fee Figaro fi Figaro foo Figaro fa Figaro Figaro Figaro!" and my father and I would howl laughing as we dried ourselves off. Louise, Danny's homely wife (people said he married her for her money), would open the door and call down, "Daniel, is that you making that racket!" He'd hold his finger to his lips, and we'd laugh the harder.

I'm still trying to figure out what lessons I learned about human relations from this band of drunks, who loved to sit on the porch in the dark with their ladies and their drinks listening to the sea, all singing together old songs like "I had a dream, dear. You had one too" or "If you were the only girl in the world/And I was the only boy." Back then, I'd feel that being grown up and having been in a war even if it wasn't the most recent one and working on Wall Street were the greatest things that could ever happen to anyone.

But now it was 1949 (or was it '48?), and Danny, holding a glass of whiskey, grabbed me one Sunday morning and accused me of filching his ginger ale out of the communal ice box when he needed it to mix with his rye. I had not taken it. Gerry, a new member of the club (who hadn't been in the war, didn't work on Wall Street, only reluctantly brought in to help with the club's finances) had given the soda to me and then gone fishing. "Liar!" Danny ripped the soda bottle out of my hands, my mouth. He poured my soda into his rye. Did he slap me?

I remember crying and running to my father, who was playing horseshoes in the strip of sand below the porch with Gus or Cookie or Harry. I told Eddie that Danny called me a thief, a liar. Eddie stopped playing horseshoes. Danny was above us on the porch.

"Your kid stole my soda. Teach your kid manners. Teach your kid not to steal, or keep the kid out of here."

Eddie turned to me.

"Did you steal it?"

"No! The drink was mine."

Eddie went up to the porch. I followed.

"Your kid's a liar."

Eddie wound up his bare hand and belted Danny so hard that blood spurted out of his mouth. Danny flew back. The drink flew up and shattered against the yellow stucco wall of the house. I remember watching my ginger ale mixed with Danny's whiskey splash out on the porch. Girl friends and wives sat up from their Adirondack chairs and then fell back so that neither the drink nor the sudden blood would spatter their summer clothes. Danny ran down the stairs. My father followed, grabbing Danny as he reached the sand. Danny got his footing and slugged my father, who slipped back in the sand. The two men—strong, in their mid-fifties, veterans of the First World War, best of friends—squared off at each other, and nobody could talk them out of their rage.

I watched, dazed, even thrilled that such a battle was being waged over the injustice done to me. Men tried to pry the two friends apart. Danny's wife ran out, screaming. My mother, who had asthma in the best of times, ran out from somewhere, screaming in disbelief at the latest disaster.

My mother rushed me upstairs to the dormitory, where the men could sleep or pass out on rows of army cots. She sat wheezing. The walls were lined with army lockers where the men kept their city clothes, their private stash. I could hear the screaming below. The smell in the air was no longer the salt of the sea. I smelled collapse. I smelled rage. I smelled embarrassment. I smelled failure. All those invisible grownup things suddenly had odors.

I looked out the window. The fight had gone out onto the narrow beach. Eddie had told me how wide the beach was when he bought the land at the auction, but in the last two decades the ocean had reclaimed a good portion of it. This was a barrier island. One day it would wash away.

People on the beach, led by Bernie the Lifeguard, tried to get in between Eddie and Danny. Umbrellas tilted. Bernie the Lifeguard's picture had been in The *Daily Mirror* one January First for going in the ocean at the stroke of midnight on New Year's Eve. I even thought Bernie the Lifeguard lived on the beach all winter. I couldn't imagine the beach without Bernie the Lifeguard protecting it. Now here was Bernie trying to rescue men, lost, not far out at sea but here on the sand.

My mother pulled me away from the window. She was furious. Her wheezing got bad. She took some medicine. Then it was quiet. Had Danny been taken off to the hospital? My father was not arrested, so I guess no police came. Did ambulances come? I don't remember. Gerry, who had given me the soda, came back from fishing and said yes indeed he had given me the soda. I wasn't a liar. There was no "Oh, I'm sorry."

The lucky part of the whole day was that my father dropped the horseshoe on his way up to finding Danny. If Eddie hadn't dropped it, he would've taken the horseshoe and surely beaten in the head of his best friend and ended up in Sing Sing, the same prison Eddie's boss, Richard Whitney, president of the New York Stock Exchange, had been sent to for embezzling the Exchange pension fund back in 1938. That was a possibility too horrible to consider. What would happen to us?

Danny was alive, and he and Louise gone. Nobody spoke to us. My mother and father and I dressed on this blandly sunny Sunday in '49 (or was it '48 or as late as '50?) and went back into the heat of town on the Long Island Railroad, empty because it was the middle of a hot day and the trains coming out from the city were still packed with people dying for a swim. We got home. Airless apartment. No one spoke. My father went into the bathroom and shut the door and ran a hot tub and stayed there for hours with his radio dangerously perched on the side of the tub and listened to songs on the radio. Nothing was said. Nothing. Ever.

Danny, my father's best friend, never came back to the beach again. The other men wrote my father a letter asking him to resign from the club. But my mother went down to the beach the next weekend and waved that letter at them and said, "None of you would be sitting here if it wasn't for Eddie coming down and buying this land and getting you all in on it. You can't do this to Eddie." So Eddie was let back in the club. But we never saw Danny again. Years later, after my father had died, I saw Danny in the street, very jaunty, still trim, with a secret smile on his face, looking like he was singing a song in his head: "Figaro Figaro." He didn't recognize me because I was no longer eleven. Or twelve. Or ten.

The club went on. Another member named Ed who lived with his sister never came back to the beach after she threw herself out the window of their apartment. Some members drifted away. Some died, as did even Bernie the Lifeguard. There was a wife swap. One Jack tricked his wife, Dorothy, and ran off with another Jack's wife, Shirley. I loved the beach. It always seemed like home. And home is the place that's sometimes the most inaccessible.

In 1973, life had reached a dead end for me. I'd had two plays produced back to back that were successes, but it didn't make life bearable. I hoped a relationship would work out, but one day, which I remember very clearly as being January 13, 1973, I knew that relationship would never work out. Never. It was over. What the hell would I do?

On that same day, I got a phone call. Would I be interested in coming to Nantucket and doing a play? Why not? And I went to Nantucket and started my life over. On a beach. Life could begin again. A new cast of characters. I invested this island—thirty miles at sea—with a sense of lost grandeur. Ralph Waldo Emerson had spoken at the Atheneum; this was Melville country. Imagine Nantucket as the whaling capital whose oil illuminated the world until some killjoy discovered kerosene in a Pennsylvania field and overnight Nantucket died. My kind of place.

I was transcendentally happy on Nantucket. We had our theater. What's the Dylan Thomas poem? "The force that through the green fuse drives the flower" was alive in me. My true life had begun. I felt Utopian.

I met the woman I would marry. I knew it the moment Adele and I met in the kitchen of an empty house. A mutual friend had gone off the island and left his house unlocked. We each went to see him, not knowing our friend wasn't on the island. I met Adele in that empty house and felt at peace in a way that I never had before. And it lasted. What happened as a result of the security of that happiness was that things I had long forgotten or buried came alive. The past became accessible. Like the day years before when my father had tried to kill his friend.

I had been writing plays about New York City, but lots of writers were writing about life in New York City, and all of us were drawing water out of the same well. I wanted a world that belonged only to me. I wanted people who spoke differently, who knew different things from the ones I knew, who didn't live now. I wanted to take away everything I knew and see what happened.

I started writing a play about a group of men who shared a war and came out of that survival with hopes for a better life. I realized I was writing about my father and his buddies. Because of the woman at the center of my life, I put a woman at the center of their lives. Both my parents' families were from New England. And here I was on Nantucket. The play would take place on Nantucket. My mother had been born in 1895. I would set the play in 1895. My mother's grandmother in Salem was named Annie Breeze. My father's grandfather in Gloucester was named Joshua Hickman; he'd been in the Civil War. That would be the war. Joshua had a number of children, including a daughter named Lydie. Put the two families together. Call the play *Lydie Breeze*. One of Joshua's daughters went off with an inventor who didn't realize he was marrying the wrong sister. Use that. I loved nineteenth-century novels. Wilkie Collins: *Armadale*, the surrealistic plotting of *Poor Miss Finch*; Hawthorne: *The Blithedale Romance* with its Utopian community and *The House of the Seven Gables* with its family curse; Melville's *Pierre* with its indescribable aura of mystery. Use these. Find a theatrical equivalent to a nineteenth-century novel. My mother's two great uncles toured vaudeville in a repertory of melodramas from 1880 to 1917. One of my characters would be an actor. What play was my actor in? That summer at Nantucket in 1973, Edward Gorey originated his production of *Dracula*. Shades of Bela Lugosi. Use that. Make my monster *Frankenstein*. Other family legends and other events in my life opened up and finally became available to me, all because of my being in Nantucket and finding Adele and wearing a mask from another century.

I first gave *Lydie Breeze* to the film director Louis Malle. We had just finishing making *Atlantic City*. He read my play and then did it beautifully at the American Place Theater in 1982. In explaining the characters to Louis, I wrote a play called *Gardenia*, which showed these people at an earlier time. Karel Reisz, the British director, directed that play in a wonderfully acted production at the Manhattan Theater Club later in 1982. I don't think I ever had a better time preparing a script than with Karel. A year or so later, James Nicola and Lloyd Rose did the two plays in tandem at a small theater in Washington, D.C. called The New Playwrights' Theatre. In seeing the two plays in one day, I realized they were not two related plays that could live independently. They were one play in two parts, a play to which I would have to return.

Years go by. In the autumn of 1999, Elizabeth Marvel, having played Blanche du Bois in a radiant and controversial production of *A Streetcar Named Desire* at the New York Theatre Workshop, mourned the powerlessness of the actor's life, saying to James Nicola, now the artistic director of the NYTW, that the cycle of an actor's life begins again—waiting for somebody to offer her a play. Jim gave her a stack of plays. "Find something for yourself in these". Among the plays were the Dramatists Play Service acting editions of *Gardenia* and *Lydie Breeze*. Elizabeth called Jim later in the week. She wanted to do a reading of these two plays. They called me and asked what I thought. "Yes!" I shouted. I said I even had rewrites on them. What had dissatisfied me about *Gardenia* was that Lydie and her crew got all this money but lacked a big dream this cash would allow them to accomplish. I thought of Lowell and the mills. I devised a plan for Lydie and the men to free the workers in those mills. The plan gave the play its true title: *Bulfinch's Mythology*. I gave Elizabeth three appearances in the second play. Jim Nicola suggested we give the plays the title *Lydie Breeze*. The second part needed a new title. I knew what it had to be: *The Sacredness of the Next Task*.

On January 24, 2000, Elizabeth cast the play with her friends. We spent a winter day and evening on East Fourth street in the East Village, watching a woman and three men on a beach in Nantucket, seeing them come together with all the best intentions in the world and seeing what happens when one of them does not put down the horseshoe but instead holds onto that horseshoe and beats his friend to death. Nicola boldly put the five-hour play into immediate production, directed by Itamar Kubovy, who had just done a play of mine at the Guthrie in Minneapolis, designed by Neil Patel, Brian McDevitt, and Gabriel Berry. Adam Guettel wrote a fantastic score. We played each part on alternate nights and then, on Saturdays and Sundays, the audience would see *Bulfinch* at 3, have dinner at 5:30, and return at 7:30 for *Sacredness*.

An angry man said to me one night: "You didn't give a credit!"

"To what?"

"What's this adapted from?"

"It isn't adapted from anything."

"This can't be a play. This has to be a novel."

Eddie. Danny. The club. Lydie. Joshua. Nantucket. I'm writing this at the Dunes Club, now in its seventieth year of existence. It's October and I'm out here with Adele closing the place up for the winter.

I can't let these people go. I'm still upstairs in that club house built out of a kit, hearing them all below, washing dishes, singing old songs, remembering a war. The sea can't ever come in to wash them away. And then I think of that day Danny pulled the soda out of my mouth and I ran to my father and nothing was ever the same again.

—John Guare
October 2000

Cast of *Lydie Breeze, Parts I and II,* directed by Itamar Kubovy and presented by James C. Nicola with scenery by Neil Patel, costumes by Gabriel Berry, lighting by Brian McDevitt, and music by Adam Guettel at the New York Theatre Workshop on May 15, 2000.

LYDIE BREEZE	Elizabeth Marvel
AMOS MASON	Boris McGiver
JOSHUA HICKMAN	Bill Camp
DAN GRADY	Matt Servitto
BEATY	Joanna P. Adler
YOUNG JEREMIAH GRADY	Scott Schmidt
O'MALLEY	Christopher McCann
LYDIE BREEZE HICKMAN	Alicia Goranson
GUSSIE HICKMAN	Alexandra Oliver
JUDE EMERSON	Thomas Shaw
JEREMIAH GRADY	Jefferson Mays
LUCIAN ROCK	Christopher McCann

Original cast of *Lydie Breeze,* directed by Louis Malle and presented by John Wulp and Roger S. Berlind with scenery by John Wulp, costumes by Willa Kim, and lighting by Jennifer Tipton at the American Place Theater on February 25, 1982.

LYDIE HICKMAN	Cynthia Nixon
BEATY	Roberta Maxwell
GUSSIE HICKMAN	Madeleine Potter
JOSHUA HICKMAN	Josef Somer
JUDE EMERSON	Robert Joy
JEREMIAH GRADY	Ben Cross
LUCIAN ROCK	James Cahill

Original cast of *Gardenia*, directed by Karel Reisz and presented by the Manhattan Theater Club with scenery by Santo Loquasto, costumes by Ann Roth, and lighting by Craig Miller on April 28, 1982.

JOSHUA HICKMAN	Sam Waterston
LYDIE BREEZE	JoBeth Williams
AMOS MASON	Edward Herrmann
DAN GRADY	James Woods
JEREMIAH GRADY	R.J. Burke
O'MALLEY	Jarlath Conroy

Part 1
Bulfinch's Mythology

ACT ONE

SCENE ONE

Nantucket, an island 30 miles off the coast of Massachusetts. 1875. June. A secluded beach on a deserted part of the island. The ocean. Beach grass. Driftwood. The house is off, over the dunes.

LYDIE BREEZE, *30s, runs on, agitated. She wears a nurse's uniform that saw duty in the Civil War. She stops, looks out at the sea and smiles. She's home. She's walked the five miles from town out along the Madeket Road. The skirt of her uniform is wet and salt-stained from walking along the sea.*

LYDIE *lies on the dune. She opens the medical bag she carries and takes out a book. She opens the book and reads:*

LYDIE

Bulfinch's Mythology.
The World and Its Origins.
By Thomas Bulfinch.

She puts the book down on her lap to see how much of it she can recite from memory:
"Before earth and sea and heaven were created, all things wore one aspect to which we give the name:
(She checks the book)
"Chaos." Oh. That. "Chaos—a confused, shapeless mass."

The next she recites from memory:

> "But God put an end to this discord. Stars began to appear.
> Fishes took possession of the sea, birds of the air, and four-
> footed beasts of the land. A nobler creature was wanted. Man
> was made! The gods gave him an upright stance so that while
> all other animals turn their faces downward and look to the
> earth, he raises his to heaven and gazes on the stars." And
> sees—
>   *(She turns the page)*
> —what? The It . . . what is the It?

She stands impatiently.

> God, give me your voice. Give me a sign. Let me hear *you.* The
> It. What is the It.

LYDIE *goes up to the house.*

The sound of the sea.

JOSHUA HICKMAN, *30s, barefoot, straw-brimmed hat, comes on from another part of the beach, a thick manuscript under one arm, reading from a book with intense concentration.*

JOSHUA

> "All spheres, grown, ungrown, small, large, suns, moons,
> planets . . . A vast similitude interlocks all . . . interlocks all . . .
> interlocks all."

JOSHUA *is off.*

The sound of the sea.

AMOS MASON, *30s, barefoot, carrying a fishing pole and bucket, comes down from the house, muttering angrily:*

AMOS

> Catch some fish. Catch some fish. Dinner tonight. Nothing in
> the larder. All bare. Mother Hubbard. Catch some fish. Catch
> some fish.

AMOS *is off to another part of the beach.*

JOSHUA *returns, even more desperate, still holding the manuscript close to him and now reciting from memory.*

JOSHUA

"All spheres, grown, ungrown, small, large, suns, moons, planets . . . A vast similitude interlocks all . . . interlocks all . . ."

JOSHUA *slumps down on the sand in despair. He places his manuscript carefully on the sand and falls back.*

LYDIE BREEZE *comes from the house down the dunes holding out a withered gardenia plant.*

LYDIE

Didn't you water the gardenia?

JOSHUA

"Interlocks all . . . a vast similitude . . ."

LYDIE

Couldn't you water it?

JOSHUA

"All spheres . . . suns . . . moons . . . planets . . ."

LYDIE

I'm gone for a week—

JOSHUA

It's gone without water for a week before.

LYDIE

A week is a long time. The world was created in a week.

JOSHUA

You go off.

LYDIE

To get us money.

JOSHUA

Oh, I can't make money.

LYDIE

This is a commune.

JOSHUA

Ah, yes. We're all equal.

LYDIE

Where's Gussie?

JOSHUA

With Amos! It's his turn to look after Gussie.

LYDIE

Why aren't you looking at me?

JOSHUA

"Suns . . . moons . . . planets."

LYDIE

It's my punishment for tending the enemy.

JOSHUA

Those people are not the enemy.

LYDIE

Those people *are* the enemy. I go into town to do my first nursing in seven years and I come home and find my gardenia plant is dead.

He turns away.

JOSHUA

It's not dead.

LYDIE

Look at it! I've had this gardenia longer than I've had you.

JOSHUA

I'm trying to read, Lydie.

LYDIE

You read. The words bury you alive.
      (*She snatches his book away.*)
What good are these words? They don't inspire you into action.
      (*She looks intently at the plant.*)
Dead. Look at it. Don't you care? I wanted my daughter to know what this plant meant. How my mother for their wedding gave my father a gardenia so he'd always have roots on this island. No matter where he sailed. Russia. Africa. And she'd tend it and nurse it while he was at sea. And finally he got

his own whaler to sail out of Nantucket and said "I christen this ship *The Gardenia* because I will always belong here no matter how far away I sail."

And he'd leave for months and come home and step off The Gardenia and the men would unload the whale oil and the clerks would pass the bonuses around and he and my mother would go off and make another baby. And we felt at the center of the world.

JOSHUA

You can still tell this to Gussie.

LYDIE

How can I explain it to her when the plant has withered and died?

JOSHUA

It's not dead.

She places the plant in front of him.

LYDIE

That? Not dead? I nurtured it. Tended it. Made it bloom during a war. Came back here. This plant was Gussie's legacy. To show her—no matter the obstacles—her mother can make things live!

JOSHUA *takes a three-page letter out of the front of the manuscript and hands it to* LYDIE.

JOSHUA

I got a letter.
    (*She takes it and reads.* JOSHUA *recites:*)
"All lives and deaths, all of the past, present, future. This vast similitude spans them and always has spann'd them. And shall forever span them and compactly hold and enclose them."

LYDIE *puts the letter down.*

LYDIE

Quite a day.

JOSHUA

Did they even read it? Aren't publishers supposed to keep manuscripts for months at a time?

LYDIE

What do they know?

JOSHUA

Atlantic Monthly? William Dean Howells? Only editor I respect? What does he know?

(JOSHUA *grabs the letter and reads:*)

"I read your manuscript with great anticipation, coming from a veteran who's founded a community dedicated to living out higher ideals since the conclusion of that tragic war. It pains me to return your voluminous manuscript to you. I suspect, sir, that you have never traveled to Europe, yet your prose is heavy with the dust of European libraries. Put it to your nose and begin sneezing! Your own past is valuable. Let the brisk air of America blow through your vigorous imagination." He goes on. "Damn it man you're an American." Blah . . . blah . . . blah.

He takes manuscript pages and flings them in the air.

LYDIE

Joshua.

JOSHUA

Is it successful in town, tending the enemy?

LYDIE

I'm so sorry.

JOSHUA

I asked you a question.

LYDIE

I made some money. We can eat.

JOSHUA

A boy enemy or a girl enemy? What did the enemy produce?

LYDIE

The baby was born—it died. It. It. Just an It.

JOSHUA

And the gardenia. *And* this letter. All things come in threes.

LYDIE

I'd hardly connect the three events.

JOSHUA

Walt Whitman says, "A vast similitude interlocks all." I thought
they'd love the book. I've been hiding out.

Silence. They embrace. Silence.

LYDIE

Have you been in the water?

JOSHUA

Still too cold.

LYDIE

It looks perfect to me.
          (*She unbuttons her jacket. She removes her corset.*)
My patient lay on her bed in labor, fully dressed. In this heat.
Gloves. Hat. A veil pulled down. Perfect go-to-meeting except,
of course, she's screaming. Do you know who my patient was?
Mrs. Clarence Sibley! The wife of the man who paid all the
bribes to win the boat contract to get to this island. When I
found out who she was I wanted to leave, but Doctor Paynter
said, "Nurse, if you want a pure action, there's nothing purer
than childbirth." I stayed. Tending the enemy.

She removes her shoes and rolls down one black stocking.

JOSHUA

Let me do the other leg.

He unrolls her stocking slowly.

LYDIE

Doctor Paynter says it's hard enough to deliver a child with the
mother naked, but to be asked to deliver a child in this fashion—and I do mean fashion. A dark maroon taffeta dress. The
husband, without looking up, said, "You may remove Mrs.
Sibley's hat. You may remove Mrs. Sibley's gloves. Mrs. Sibley's
dress stays on." Do each toe, Joshua.

JOSHUA

I will, I will.

She removes her skirt. She sits on the sand in her camisole and petticoat.

LYDIE

The wife says to me, "Nurse, Mr. Sibley likens my body to the temple at Jerusalem built by King David, and down there where my child is"—she had to stop because the labor pains came back. After, "Down there where my child is I liken to the Inner Temple, and my child is the Ark of the Covenant, and in front of this most sacred of places, the priests have hung a veil, sacred. Not to be touched. Not to be seen." Then she began screaming again. Doctor Paynter tried to rip her skirt off, but the husband leaped up and held Doctor Paynter back. "All right," said Doctor Paynter. All right. I've never heard two words packed with more contempt. And we began to deliver Mrs. Sibley's child, reaching up under the soaking maroon skirts. Not white, but maroon so the blood wouldn't be noticed. I felt a head on my fingers and the umbilical cord. And the blood was weighing down the crinolines and the taffeta so it was like working under plaster of Paris. Keep rubbing my legs. It feels so good. This sun feels so good. Maybe the gardenia will be saved.

JOSHUA

Relax. Relax.

LYDIE

Mr. Sibley told us they wanted to name their first-born child Forbearance or Perspicacity. Some Puritan virtue. Dr. Paynter and I ripped the skirt back to get the baby out from under the maroon. Too late. The umbilical cord had tightened around the child's throat. They can call this baby Eternity.

JOSHUA

You mustn't blame yourself.

LYDIE

I looked up. Saw a portrait of Ulysses S. Grant nailed over the bed. The husband was weeping, but he said, so proudly, "President Grant sent me his picture. We wish he'd run a third term." I stopped, my hands still red with her blood. "You support Grant's third term in office? You support the butcher of Cold Harbor? You didn't hear the boys dying at Cold Harbor? You didn't see that mountain of corpses—thousands and thousands of men dead, men who are sacred—all wasted, thanks to your precious Ulysses S. Grant. And you mourn for one little baby? This—you mourn for this? You haven't seen what I have seen. I suppose you support strengthening Grant's military? I suppose you support Grant's corruption? No wonder your baby died!" Doctor Paynter threw the basin against the wall and asked me to leave.

I don't think he'll be requiring my nursing talents any more. He'll get the child off to the bone ferry. Sail off Nantucket down the River Styx.

JOSHUA

Undo your hair. You're home.

He takes the combs from her hair. He loosens her hair.

LYDIE

Yes. Back here. This beach. This sand. If I squint my eyes, that could be my father out there in the water. *The Gardenia* setting sail. No time. No motion. No change. This gardenia could even be blooming. You're there beginning your book. I'm asking the right questions. I'm finding the right answers. "God put an end to this discord. Stars began to appear . . . A nobler creature was wanted. Man was made." We're all just beginning. You. Me. Amos. Dan Grady. Has Dan Grady written? Do we know where he is?

JOSHUA

He's chugging around the country. Punching tickets. We've seen the last of Dan Grady.

LYDIE

You think?

JOSHUA

Vanished like smoke. Railroad smoke.

LYDIE

I won't mind that. It's always better when it's just the two of us.

JOSHUA

Well—Amos.

LYDIE

Only Amos.

JOSHUA

Now, Lydie, don't get all down in the mouth or I'll think you're pregnant. You're not pregnant. Are you?
      (LYDIE *walks away.*)
You got like this when you were pregnant with Gussie. No. I mustn't torment myself. You couldn't be pregnant. How long has it been since we've made love? I've never stopped loving you. It's just this book—this damned pile of pages. It's drained me. We'll begin again. I've let you down badly. No. You're not pregnant.

LYDIE

Don't torment yourself.

JOSHUA

We're still living in winter.

LYDIE

And summer not here yet.

JOSHUA

And you nursing. Tending the enemy.

LYDIE

And the book.

JOSHUA

And Gussie's teeth coming in.

LYDIE

And the shutters.

JOSHUA

The cow wandered away.

JOSHUA *kisses* LYDIE *deeply. A moment. She bursts out laughing. She takes off her petticoat.*

LYDIE

What I want to know is how did that husband in town get in there in the first place?

JOSHUA

He must've sneaked into the foreground of the Inner Temple one ocean-black night.

LYDIE

Lifted up the veil. He shines his lantern inside.

JOSHUA

A wind blows.

LYDIE

An army of Vestal Virgins all looking like Ulysses S. Grant stands inside her womb. "May we help you?"

JOSHUA

I'd like to come in.

LYDIE

Pay us bribes. Pay us graft.

JOSHUA

I'll pay. I'll pay.

They embrace and fall to the ground. She pulls away.

LYDIE

Why did we ever get married?

JOSHUA

We married because the police wouldn't let us live here together unless you were married to either Dan Grady or Amos or me.

LYDIE

My first compromise.

JOSHUA

You made the right choice. I loved you the most.

LYDIE

Marriage. Weren't we going to show the world our contempt for its institutions? Didn't we plan manifestoes? Aipotu . . . Why did we want to spell Utopia backwards?

JOSHUA

I'm so glad you're back. Bring the patients here, but don't stay away for such a long time.

LYDIE

Is Gussie all right?

JOSHUA

Amos is walking with her.

LYDIE

Are her teeth hurting her?

JOSHUA

We did what you said.

LYDIE

Put the raisin in the cheesecloth?

JOSHUA

You can even see where Gussie's little teeth are coming in. The tiny slash of white against that pink gum. She bit down on the cheesecloth and the raisin and went floating off to sleep. Maybe we should leave the island. Move to New York or Boston.

LYDIE

No.

JOSHUA

Maybe our moment of glory came in the moment we dreamed it.

LYDIE

No.

JOSHUA

The three men at Cold Harbor. Amos. Dan Grady. Joshua. Lydie Breeze, our nurse. The carnage. Thousands of men dead in moments. Charge! No supplies. No hope. U.S. Grant gone mad. If we go back into that battle, we will die. Where to go? "I know an island," the nurse sings. I swear you sang it, sang those words. "I know an island." The nurse would read to us from Shakespeare, and I'd heard of Shakespeare but never saw a play by Shakespeare, but by the time I did, I said, Ahhh, I knew all of Shakespeare the minute I heard that nurse say, "I know an island." All of Shakespeare. You men can't be defeated.

LYDIE

You men can't be defeated.

JOSHUA

I have a house, she sang. Thirty miles off the coast of America. We'll write manifestoes and develop a society that will shine as a beacon to the world. A paradise of the mind. A garden of Eden.

LYDIE

And we did it!

JOSHUA

Not yet.

LYDIE

We *shall* do it.

JOSHUA

Oh Lydie, you still have hope?

LYDIE

We shall do it.

JOSHUA

That shutter still swinging loose up there.

LYDIE

A race of titans.

JOSHUA

But isn't collapse a condition of Eden?

LYDIE

This community, warts and all, is going to stand. We'll find the magnet that will pull us together. The It. The It. The Great Idea.

JOSHUA

Lydie, in the war, we'd reach a point like this and retrench.
Reconsider. Regroup.

LYDIE

You've finished your book. Pregnancy. Melancholy. Pregnancy.
Melancholy. We can't let it reach up and drag us down. We
have to fight the current.

JOSHUA

The last seven years . . .
Pause.

LYDIE

Now what we are going to do is this. I am going up and look at
my baby. Amos must be back by now with her. Bathe my baby.
Feed her. You are going to help. You will find the cow. Milk it.
I will make a dinner cooked with whatever shreds I find in the
garden. You will read to me from "Bulfinch's Mythology. The
Creation of the World"—If we could show men what they
could be—is this the idea—is this the It? To make a play out of
"Bulfinch's Mythology" and take it—where? To those mills in
Lawrence, in Lowell, and free the workers chained to the
machines. Take our play to the mills? Get in somehow. I believe
this: Art must change the world or it's not art. Show this new
breed of slaves that they are the mirror of man's greatness.

JOSHUA

Goddamn it, Lydie! Seven years I plow away on my book.
Seven years! William Dean Howells sends it back! Maybe I
should put out to sea. Get to Europe. Suppose the letter is
right. I've never been to Europe. I don't know anything. I
make it all up in my head. I thought if I swam to the bottom of
myself I could come back to the surface with a treasure that
would be truly original. I wanted to startle the world. I get
back a letter from the smartest man in America, who *scoffs* at
me. Suppose he's right? *Bulfinch's Mythology*? The Golden
Age? We were supposed to find our destiny here—

LYDIE

But this is an idea—

JOSHUA

Ideas need money. Go off the island and free workers? We couldn't even afford a ferry ride off this godforsaken—"I know an island." I know despair.

LYDIE

Money. Money. Wait, I have an idea! Yes. Now don't say No before you hear it. We have all this room in the house. Instead of traveling to Europe—no matter what our plan is we'll need money—while we plan our strategy we'll need money. How to get money? We need time to plan a strategy. Use the summer for that. Freedom in the autumn. Autumn is the best time for freedom. The summer is for making money. We'll bring people to us. And charge them—Yes! We'll take people in for the summer.

JOSHUA

A boarding house? We didn't begin this community to turn it into a boarding house!

LYDIE

We could *advertise* for people interested in a life of the mind. People who want to get away from the cares of the city for the summer. Join an apostolic society. No, that's no good. It sounds religious. A fraternity. Join men and women interested in a life of the mind but while getting into closer contact with nature and work. We can advertise in learned journals. We might get some very interesting people who have money. People who've been to Europe and can spend it here! People who laugh at William Dean Howells. I see wonderful dinners on a long table looking down at the sea.

JOSHUA

This is the way I like you!

LYDIE (*Formal*)

How do we unchain ourselves from history without losing any of the value from the past? More codfish?

JOSHUA (*Formal*)

By making ourselves worthy of the great secret forces in life. Pass the piccalilli relish?

LYDIE

Yes! To be worthy of this remarkable planet! We've been through wars. We could've been killed. But we survived it all. Even the poverty now. There is a great plan for us. On this beach. Under this sky. Waiting for the secret to unlock it all. Say yes? It's an interim measure to bring in money.

JOSHUA

Fine. It's some action. Yes! Dear Lydie, we shall find that key. Here. On this beach. In this house. Under this sky. Whatever our solutions will be, they will be here. Not a railroad track. Dan Grady. Chugging away.

LYDIE

(Kicking the plant.)

The gardenia. Throw it away. Not worth a snap. Just a plant. Almost a weed. The human spirit. That's the real show.

JOSHUA

And we'll begin our life together as hotel keepers. Go upstairs. Get into our bed. We might even start a new child. This is the first pragmatic thing we've done since we've been here.

LYDIE

Is that Amos down there?

JOSHUA

A daughter. To name after you.

LYDIE

Is that Amos fishing? Why is Amos Mason fishing? Amos?

JOSHUA

He can't hear you.

LYDIE *(Calling)*

Amos!

JOSHUA

The surf is too high.

LYDIE

You said he was walking the baby. Where is she?

JOSHUA

She must be asleep. He tiptoed off. She is almost a year old.

LYDIE

And that's old enough to leave?

JOSHUA

A year old! Don't you hear me? We'll start a new child!

LYDIE

What is wrong with you? What asylum have I committed myself to?

JOSHUA

Go up to the house! I bet the baby's fine!
    (LYDIE *runs up the dune to the house.*)
I'll cut the gardenia back! I'll find green!

JOSHUA *goes after her, holding the dead plant.* AMOS *comes on, carrying a bucket. He's been surf-casting.* AMOS *has a slight speech impediment, which is enough to make even those who love him treat him as a buffoon.*

AMOS

Were you yelling at me?

JOSHUA

You left the damned baby? You've upset Lydie.

AMOS

Gussie was snoring. I've never heard a year-old baby snore. Very loud. Very peaceful. I went down to the water.

JOSHUA *(Calls)*

Lydie, the baby's safe!

AMOS *(Angry)*

Stuck my line in the surf. Dinner tonight. Nothing in the larder. All gone. Mother Hubbard. I'm watching the line from here.

JOSHUA

We have very exciting news. Freeing the slaves in the mills over in Lowell! Lydie has a plan. Doing a play that will show the workers the desolation of their lives! Amos, it's going to take some doing on our parts at first.

AMOS

How do we get there? We don't have money to buy a mule.

JOSHUA

We are freeing ourselves. We're going to extend the community. It's this. Take in guests this summer. Charge a fortune! We have the barn. Turn that into rooms.

AMOS

That ramshackle—

JOSHUA

That primitiveness we'll advertise as part of the charm of the place. People who want to get away from the city—Advertise in only the finest magazines. "The Atlantic Monthly."

AMOS

Why?

JOSHUA

We should be associating with people who live a life of the mind.

AMOS

By advertising for them?

JOSHUA

I realize you've been working hard putting the new roof on the house, but I'll help you remodel the barn—

AMOS

And minding the baby. Climbing down off the roof every time she cries because you're locked in your room—

JOSHUA

Work of the mind is as exhausting as—

AMOS

Lydie Breeze is off in town—

JOSHUA

Nursing to get us money so we can eat—

AMOS

We came here to share and you and Lydie Breeze are sharing
a bed at night, getting married, filling up the ideal community
with all the babies in the world, screaming and making me a
nanny.

JOSHUA

Gussie is not all the babies in the world.

AMOS

And now you want to make me a bellhop? I have bullet
wounds and I end up a nanny? And a bellhop? The bellhop
of the sand dunes. I may be scarred, but I didn't get shot in
the head.

JOSHUA

It's just an interim measure to get money that will allow us—

AMOS

Opening a hotel? We came up here to begin an ideal community—

JOSHUA

The solution is not perfect, but do you want all our work to
wash out to sea?

AMOS

To expand our minds.

JOSHUA

And we have.

AMOS

To help you write your *magnum opus*.

JOSHUA

And you have.

AMOS

We don't have any *money*! We used all our money to repair this
house. We don't have any money for books.

JOSHUA

Nantucket has one of the finest libraries—

AMOS

We've read every book in the *Atheneum*! I have all this knowledge in my head. I don't know how to use it, apply it.

JOSHUA

This is a tantrum. You're having a tantrum.

AMOS

We had this fantasy—

JOSHUA

Dream!

AMOS

—*fantasy* we'd be examples of a higher life. We had this fantasy.

JOSHUA

Dream! What's wrong with you.

AMOS

That we could teach ourselves.

JOSHUA

A dream that is fast becoming reality. Lydie has this idea—Bulfinch—to show the glory of man! Yes! We'll put our lives at risk—Go into the mills! But we shall succeed, and when we do that, we'll be recognized as true vital intellectuals, not today's brainless variety who worship Darwin without understanding the first thing about Darwin. It's not about strength. It's about adaptability—

AMOS

Joshua.

JOSHUA

Blessing human greed with the scientific name of evolution is no answer.

AMOS

Joshua!

JOSHUA

When my book is published—

AMOS

Joshua!

JOSHUA

I am already engaged in correspondence with men the caliber
of William Dean Howells. I am getting letters from—

AMOS

I saw the letter from William Dean Howells.

JOSHUA

You can't read my mail! An ideal community has principles.

AMOS

We fought a war against false and cruel principles. To show
men could not be bought or sold. And I end up gardening and
pickling watermelon rinds to sell in town to make money to
live out these principles? That's an example of purity? To end
up being a nanny to a child not even mine? We were supposed
to examine the purposes of being male and female, but I didn't
think I'd become a woman. And now a bellhop! The search for
something higher? Lightning rods for a greater evolution?
Seven years now. Did you lie to yourself? Didn't you know
your book wasn't any good?

JOSHUA

Oh, yes, I kept after it all these years—these Sisyphus years—
pushing my worthless rock up infinite hills.

AMOS

Are you serious?

LYDIE *appears at the top of the dune carrying a straw basket that holds
Gussie, her sleeping infant.*

LYDIE

Irony, dear Amos. That's irony.

*She sets down the basket and places her straw hat against it as a parasol.
She signals them not to wake the baby.*

JOSHUA

Amos is being so supportive. He knows all about the book's reception. He's being a brick about it.

AMOS

I'll tell you what's ironic. Me peeling potatoes to the music of your pen scrawling away after our immortality. I'm so exhausted trying to keep this meager farm alive. My labor produces no music. I can't think. My brain is cauliflower and cabbage and weeds. While you were writing your book, we all had a mission. We could see ourselves reflected in the glow of your genius. Well, the mirror's broken. The irony is now we've had our seven years of bad luck before the mirror broke. Everything's backwards at Aipotu.

LYDIE

Seven years to hive up this bitter honey.

JOSHUA

We came up here to heal ourselves.

AMOS

And we have.

JOSHUA

And now it's time to move on?

AMOS

I didn't say that.

LYDIE

But what do you say, Amos?

AMOS

I've said quite enough.

LYDIE *takes a package out of the basket and holds it behind her back.*

LYDIE

Are you leading a secret life?

AMOS

A secret life?

LYDIE

Do you creep out your window at night?

AMOS

I am beaten down by this life. I promised myself I'd finish "The Decline and Fall of the Roman Empire" by summer. I'm lucky if I can make it through the Farmer's bleeding Almanac. A secret life? Are you serious?

JOSHUA

Secrets?

LYDIE

I went looking for my rouge, Joshua. To put some color in these faded cheeks. I looked everywhere. I finally found it.

She unfolds a soft leather loincloth and a feathered headdress. She tosses a tin of rouge to JOSHUA. AMOS *grabs for it.*

LYDIE

I found this in the pantry. Newly packed and wrapped.

JOSHUA *snatches the loincloth.*

AMOS

Give me that!

JOSHUA *takes the Indian headdress.*

JOSHUA

Feathers? A loin cloth?

JOSHUA *puts them on.*

AMOS

That's mine.

LYDIE

A tin of my rouge? Do you think Amos is serious? He is becoming a woman. Won't Amos look beautiful in a bustle?

AMOS

I want those!

LYDIE

Are you becoming an actor?
> (JOSHUA *runs up and down the beach doing an
> Indian dance.* AMOS *follows.*)

Are you joining a circus?

AMOS

I need those in town. Joshua!

JOSHUA *tosses the loincloth to* LYDIE.

LYDIE

Joining the sock and buskin? A band of merry players?

JOSHUA

You know what these are, Lydie? Amos won these feathers in
a dice game. Indians in Kentucky were selling off their treasures. Hee-chatta. Ho-chatta. Hee-chatta. Ho-chatta.

AMOS

I want those feathers back.

JOSHUA

You're going to join a new tribe?

AMOS

Fete Day. The Congregational Church is having a Fete Day.

JOSHUA

Fate Day?

LYDIE

Your fate is going to be with the Congregational Church?

AMOS

Not Fate. Fete!

LYDIE

Fate as in Kismet?

JOSHUA

Fate as in Destiny?

AMOS

Fete as in fancy French. A festival. No destiny. Everybody's going to dress up and recreate the early days of life on this island. I've been thinking about it and I've decided I want to get involved in the life of the town.

LYDIE

Politics?

AMOS *(Stuttering)*

Politics.

LYDIE

Work your way up to the Senate? Join the Millionaire's Club?

AMOS

Maybe it's time for decent men to get into politics.

LYDIE

We'll hang a portrait of Ulysses S. Grant over your bed.

AMOS

We're trapped out here.

JOSHUA

And to escape, you run off to join a Congregational Church Fete Day.

AMOS

I'm descending off Mount Olympus and putting on feathers and joining a pageant and maybe I'll meet someone. A woman.

LYDIE

A fisherman's daughter.

AMOS

You were a fisherman's daughter.

LYDIE

The difference between whales and bluefish is immense.

JOSHUA

Don't let Lydie's red rouge scare her off.

AMOS *(Uneasy)*

I want to meet people at the bank. Get on their good side.

(Pause.)

Maybe the bank would like to buy out my share in the house.

Pause.

LYDIE

You'll take your share out of the house?

AMOS

I could go to Harvard.

JOSHUA

Amos Mason at Harvard?

LYDIE *(Old voice)*

Hello? Speak up, I'm the oldest freshman in the freshman class.

JOSHUA *(Old voice)*

You must be Amos Mason.

AMOS

I wrote to the Law School. I could go there.

JOSHUA

If. If. There's always an If.

AMOS

If I have the tuition.

LYDIE

And if you had the knowledge. When I found you at Cold Harbor, you could barely read or write.

AMOS

I would be accepted because of what I've learned here.

LYDIE

How would you pay for it?

AMOS

I have a share in the house.

LYDIE

I gave you a share in the house.

AMOS

That was very noble of . . . Don't make this hard . . . You'd . . .

LYDIE

Speak up. Speak up!

AMOS

You'd buy me out.

JOSHUA

With what?

AMOS

I thought—I was hoping—they'd publish your book. *Prolego-mena To Duty*. And it would be published all over the world in millions of copies and translated into languages we didn't even know. Malayo-Polynesian. Hindustani. French.

JOSHUA

So that was behind all your good wishes.

AMOS

I wanted your book to be published for all of us. I loved when you'd read to us from the book. All the talk about people being like planets and how we had to make up new universes. Hearing universal harmonies. That a great book would come out of our community. That would be sold all over the world.

JOSHUA

And with that money?

AMOS

You'd buy me out.

JOSHUA

So you could go to Harvard.

AMOS

So I could go to Harvard.

LYDIE

An Indian at Harvard.

AMOS

I'm no Indian. My people are from Virginia.

JOSHUA

Do they bribe you to be in the pageant?

AMOS

They promise you five cents. To cover expenses.

JOSHUA

How many sins are blanketed in the name of covering expenses?

LYDIE

My God, you can be had for five cents.

AMOS

We came up to this island to lead exemplary lives. How can we lead exemplary lives if everyone's laughing at us? I give our address in town and people still laugh. "Aipotu. Is that Utopia spelled backwards?" "That's right." "Do you folks do every-thing backwards out there? We notice you do the planting all wrong. Do you all talk backwards and think backwards and for-nicate backwards and eat backwards and shit backwards so it goes into your brains? Aipotu? A good name for you all."

JOSHUA

Is that what they say?

LYDIE

It's always so easy to scoff at any higher purpose.

AMOS

You may have a transcendental purpose. Joshua may have a transcendental purpose. I don't have a transcendental purpose. I came up here to get a transcendental purpose. To share. And you don't even consult me about the name of the fraternity. Aipotu. You said we were all equals. And you never even asked me for my choice of a name. The Oasis. I wanted to call it the Oasis. No one would laugh at us if we called it the Oasis.

JOSHUA

You've been letting this stew for seven years?

AMOS

Dan Grady suggested Arcadia. But, no, the two of you make all
the decisions. I wouldn't have minded Arcadia. People don't
laugh at Arcadia. Or the Forest of Arden. Arden.

JOSHUA

Did you know he was unhappy with the name?

LYDIE

I didn't know he was unhappy with the name.

JOSHUA

I thought we all agreed on Aipotu.

LYDIE

I loved Aipotu.

JOSHUA

Sounded Indian.

LYDIE

Contained a secret.

JOSHUA

I'm proud to give my address as Aipotu.

AMOS

My only pride these past seven years is you are here writing a
treatise on the transcendental purpose of life and I am part of
that endeavor and when it is published and the tumultuous
roar quiets the great men of the universe will flock to our community—not a rooming house—but a model for the ages. I
endured all the impossible winters and unending summers
because we were building a hothouse for these orchids that
would bloom out of your head.

LYDIE

Gardenia. That's the flower of today.

JOSHUA

William Dean Howells is not the only publisher. I'll send the
book out again. Change my sights. Lower my sights. Just a bit.

AMOS

No! You told me never to lower our sights. Not a tad.

JOSHUA

Sticking by me has made you a saint.

AMOS

But I won't be a martyr.

JOSHUA

We could call the community Calvary. Amos's Calvary.

AMOS

Sahara. That would be the proper name for this—what?
Rooming house? That's what we've become?

JOSHUA *(Furious)*

The book is rejected. What am I supposed to do? Kill myself?

AMOS

Will it do any good? Will it give me back seven years? Will it
make your book worth publishing? Will your death get me
into Harvard? We've had everything at this community but a
death. A child born. Crops harvested. Blizzards. Floods. Oh
yes. A book written. A brilliant book written. Seven years waiting to reap that harvest. Will your death give me back seven
years? If it would, then I want you dead. My God! Finally! I
have a transcendental idea. Yes, Joshua, I want your death. In
exchange for my life. We all have one good idea in us.

JOSHUA, *stunned, looks at him.* JOSHUA *goes up the dune. He is gone.*

LYDIE *(Furious)*

I earned the titanic sum of four dollars in town. Buy that
fisherman's daughter a cool drink of tonic. One dollar. One
quarter share.

She flings the bill down on the sand.

AMOS

I'm sorry, Lydie. I don't want to give Joshua any pain. Explain
to him.

LYDIE

Explain what to him?

AMOS

Why I'm going to town.

LYDIE

You've made yourself quite clear.

AMOS

I'm sorry.

He begins crying.

LYDIE

Explain what? There is no choice. Let your loneliness lead you into town and let your loneliness join you up to the men who find their perfect god in presidents like Ulysses S. Grant. Give in to your loneliness and let your loneliness make you a spoke in the wheel of the machine that spews out human beings like Carnegie and Jay Gould and this new man, Rockefeller. Or stay here where the road is not strewn with joy, but where you shall find true heroism. Heroism to resist the doubt. Heroism to keep true to the ideals of justice. Not to be a precious gardenia that needs tending or it shall wither and die. Not to blossom without the water. To find the water in our hearts! We shall flower, Amos, whether you go into town or not. The path to town is that way. Your loneliness must know the way there. I hope you can find your way back.

AMOS *looks at her. He picks up his gear, his feathers. He starts to go off. He stoops to pick up the bill and goes.* LYDIE *lies on the dune. She stares at the sea. The baby cries.* LYDIE *leans over the basket and comforts her child:*

LYDIE *(Sings)*

"When I was a child
And you were a child
In a kingdom by the sea . . ."
A secret. Do you want to know a secret? Dr. Paynter examined me in town. Do you want a little brother? Do you want a little sister?
      (Sings:)
"Many a year ago
In a kingdom by the sea . . ."

LYDIE *falls back in despair. Then a voice calls:*

> DAN *(off)*
> Somebody should tell Amos to check his line.

> LYDIE
> Don't even talk to me, Dan Grady.

DAN GRADY, *30s, appears at the top of the dune, holding* AMOS's *fishing rod, a live fish dangling from it. He carries a canvas duffel bag over one shoulder. He wears a conductor's cap. He's barefoot, dressed in clean white trousers, looking remarkably refreshed and clean.*

> DAN
> Amos's rod being pulled into the sea.

> LYDIE
> You said you'd be back last month.

> DAN
> But I rescued it.

> LYDIE
> I had you in derailments.

> DAN
> Safe and sound.

> LYDIE
> Indians holding you up.

> DAN
> Oh yes—lots of Indians.

> LYDIE
> I had you being tortured.

> DAN
> Hee-chatta, ho-chatta.

> LYDIE
> Skin being pulled back.

> DAN
> Hee-chatta, ho-chatta.

LYDIE

Scalped hair by hair.

DAN

Ouch.

LYDIE

Hot coals put under your eyelids.

DAN

I could take that.

LYDIE

Buried in a mound of red ants.

DAN

I hear that's very cooling.

LYDIE

Hungry red ants.

DAN

Very refreshing.

LYDIE

You were faithful to me?

DAN

As only I can be.

LYDIE

Whatever that means.

DAN

We train conductors take an oath of chastity.

LYDIE

I'd like to see that.

DAN

The Union Pacific administers the vows. If you check Clause
Twenty-eight of the Interstate Commerce Act, you will see list-
ed all the penalties for any unlawful breakage of the laws of
Faithfiality.

LYDIE

Faithfiality?

DAN

That's the legal word for chastity.

LYDIE

Faithfiality? Faithful to the initial impulse. That seems to be the hardest thing for a human being to do. Faithfiality. Faithfiality. Don't be so cheery. It drives me mad.

DAN

I haven't forgotten.

LYDIE

Forgotten what? You can't even remember my address.

DAN

I live here too.

LYDIE

You don't live here. You live on two parallel iron tracks on a metal thing that shoots out plumes of smoke. Human cargo. We'll let out long lonely whistles in the night so you'll feel at home in the brief time you're here. I have to go up. You can clean that fish.

She goes up the dune.

DAN

I've quit the railroad. I've got in touch with Jeremiah. I want him with me here. With us. His grandparents will be glad to get rid of him.

LYDIE

You're bringing your seven-year-old son here?

DAN

I'm as much a share holder in this house as anyone. You ask me where I live? Here, Lydie. Here.

LYDIE

I can't take care of another child.

DAN

Not asking you to. I met a little Irish girl on the ferry.

LYDIE

I don't want to hear the carnal adventures of Dan Grady—

DAN

She was looking for work. I told her we could use a nurse to look after the children.

LYDIE

How can we afford a nurse?

DAN

Beaty's her name. She'll be here in a while.

LYDIE

You don't know what's happened to me.

DAN

Her name is Beaty.

LYDIE

You go away, and I think I've gone mad wondering where you are because you don't realize what's happened to me.

DAN

Now, I realize that work is prayer and that's the basis of this community, but it won't hurt to hire a little scullery girl to do some of the baser praying for us. She'll cook and clean and free you. Free us all. For higher things.

He touches her face.

LYDIE

You should wait for the effects of the opium to diminish before you make your annual appearance here.

DAN

If you're going up to the house, stick these down the well?

He opens the duffel bag and produces two bottles of wine.

LYDIE

Champagne?

DAN

And this other one's Vouvray. I ordered cases of it. The man in
New York said it goes good with fish. And here I am rescuing
fish out of the sea. And in some Balzac novel you read to me
they were always drinking champagne. Haven't you always
wondered what the devil champagne tasted like? Tonight we
shall find out. Is Joshua still scribbling away at his master-
piece? Could we pry him loose long enough to go over to the
fishmonger's and get some soft-shell crabs? I passed by a great
blue stack of the beautiful things. I have hot sauce from
Louisiana down in my bag. Are you paralyzed, Lydie?

LYDIE

Joshua's book was rejected by the publisher.

DAN

Then I'll publish it. How much can it cost to publish a book?

LYDIE

It breaks my heart to see you mad.

DAN

Send Joshua off to the fishmonger's! Do you hear me? I want
time alone with you.

LYDIE

The bottom fell out, and we're all in this hole.

DAN *removes the fish from* AMOS's *line.*

DAN

Let's ask this fish if he thinks we're in a hole. He swims around
the sea. He sees what's going on. He's on the brink of evolution, deciding whether to quit the sea and move up here with
us. He's investigated this area.
    (*He does a ventriloquist act with the fish.*)
Fish? This damsel thinks she's in a hole. "Dig a hole to get out
of a hole."

*He walks the fish around the beach like a water seeker with a dowsing
stick.*

LYDIE

Come up to the house. Dan. Please.

The fish begins shaking violently.

DAN

The fish says dig here! This is a command!
> (DAN *kneels and digs feverishly in the sand. He uncovers a black Gladstone bag.*)

"What could this be?" asks the fish. Shut up, fish. Don't speak unless spoken to. Back into the sea! No more evolution for you!
> (*He opens the bag.* LYDIE *comes closer. He spills out cash.*)

I always felt pirates landed here. Or was it the Spanish Armada? No. No gold doubloons. This swagger is dollar bills. Five-dollar bills. Ten-dollar bills. Twenties. Fifties. Excellent pirates.
> (*He hands* LYDIE *a stack of bills. She falls to her knees.*)

LYDIE

Where did this come from?

DAN

I can taste those soft-shell crabs.

LYDIE

What have you done?

DAN

You pop them in the pan over high heat. Butter! We have to buy butter! Can they take a hundred-dollar bill at the dairy? Toss the crabs in. A snootful of paprika. Cut up the parsley. Turn them over. Slide them out onto plates. My late wife must have had a trace of Hungarian in her, or else why would she use paprika? I wonder if my son will demand paprika on all his food? He'll be here. Everything is here. Lydie. I'm home.

LYDIE *is petrified.* DAN *embraces her.*

SCENE TWO

Carousing voices: "Story! Story! Story! Tell us the story."

Evening. Full moon. LYDIE, JOSHUA *and* DAN *are lit by the campfire on the beach. Wine bottles, pots and pans in which they've cooked their feast, are littered around the fire.* LYDIE *and* JOSHUA *applaud.*

LYDIE

Story! Story!

DAN *bows, with a theatrical flourish.*

DAN

The Adventures of Dan Grady!
            (LYDIE *and* JOSHUA *cheer.*)
In our latest chapter, our hero Dan Grady, as usual in the past five hundred chapters, is riding the rails, punching tickets, watching the scenery go by, waiting to come back here.

LYDIE

I don't want any fiction.

DAN

Dan Grady overhears two voices *deeeep* in a discussion as he starts to knock on the door of their compartment. Outside the window, Illinois passes by. Dan Grady hears angry words. "Washington, D.C." "I was there first." "I was there first." Whistles blow. Ohio passes by the window. "Stockholders' rights." "*My* stockholders' rights." Chugga-chugga-chugga. Black smoke blocks out the view. "I have Congress in my pocket." The other voice says, "I have somebody much bigger in my pocket." Who is bigger than Congress? The whistle blows. I can't hear. Maybe I will see about publishing Joshua's book. How much can it cost?

JOSHUA

You're telling us a story.

DAN

Late that night, our hero Dan Grady's buzzer is buzzed from

the compartment. Dan Grady struggles down through the cars of the sleeping passengers, sleeping behind dark maroon curtains, feeling he's in a dream. He gets to that compartment. He opens the door. This is what Dan Grady sees. The two men still sitting there. A whiskey bottle between them, empty. A man with a Gladstone bag on his lap clutches his heart. Trying to loosen his collar. I've seen heart attacks before. But I've never seen heart attacks with their heart in one hand and a smoking pistol in the other. The other man—glen-plaid suit—diamond stick pin—is slumped back in his chair, a bloodstain on his shirt front. The heart-attack man says, "I never shot a man. I never shot a man." The glen-plaid shot man says "Well, he shot *me*. He shot *me*." They each reach out to me. Each. Reach. To me. "Help *me*." "Help *me*."

LYDIE

I don't like this story. Scare. Scare. Scare.

DAN

Two dying men battling each other. Froth at their mouths. Heavy breathing. Blood from the shot man transferring to the heart-attack man's white shirt front.

LYDIE

Scare. Scare. Scare.

DAN

They fall on each other at the same moment. Stop. Still. Quiet. Ooooooooooo! Chugga-chugga-chugga. Then the train whistle screams again. Ooooooooooo! I lock the door. I go to open the Gladstone bag to see what was in it. The heart-attack man opens his eyes. "Curse. Curse. Put that bag down. Curse." His arm fell. And this time he was dead.

JOSHUA

He cursed this bag?

DAN

I take the bag out and hide it in my locker. "Murder! Murder!" The colored fella from the kitchen was going up the train announcing breakfast, and he must have opened their door because he kept hollering "Murder! Murder!" the same way he'd been yelling "Breakfast! Breakfast!"

Police got on at the next stop. The police said it was all simple. Two representatives of rival railroads going to Washington to do some lobbying.

JOSHUA

They let you go? The bag. This bag. A curse?

DAN

Dan Grady gets off at Washington, where the run was ending anyway, and checks into a hotel. He looks at the side of his new Gladstone bag.
(DAN *holds the bag against the fire light. He points out letters:*)
D.A.R.T.A.G.N.A.N.

JOSHUA

D'Artagnan!

LYDIE

The Three Musketeers!

DAN

Porthos. Athos. Aramis. Me. Joshua. Amos. You were D'Artagnan, Lydie. You were our leader. All for one. One for all. I opened the bag. Well, you see the money.

LYDIE

All the way down to the bottom?

JOSHUA

The money goes all the way down . . .

DAN

In smaller letters. See? It's written "Casa Blanca." I sit in the hotel room and stare and stare at it. See this. See how certain letters in D'Artagnan are underlined. See that? 'A' is underlined.

LYDIE

A.R.T.G.N.

DAN

I keep staring at the letters. They rearrange themselves in my brain. Try it. Rearrange the underlined ones. I think of rainy nights here on Nantucket. Us playing anagrams.

LYDIE

T.R. No—G.N.

JOSHUA

No. Try G.R.

LYDIE

I'm no good at this!

DAN

G.R.

LYDIE

A.N.T.

DAN

G.R.A.N.T. And Casa Blanca. Now anybody knows enough Spanish for that.

LYDIE & JOSHUA

House. White. Grant. Grant. White House. Ulysses S. Grant? The White House!

DAN

The voices of the two men. "I have the Congress sewed up." "I have somebody bigger."

LYDIE

Ulysses S. Grant.

JOSHUA

This money was destined for the White House.

DAN

You know what I did?

LYDIE

I don't want to hear this. I'm scared. Pull up the covers. Scare. Scare.

DAN

I went over to the White House. Strolled right over to Sixteen Hundred Pennsylvania Avenue. Even asked a policeman for directions. Asked the guard at the White House. I sauntered up and said, "Excuse me, sir. But I had a package for D'Artagnan." His eyes opened. "You wait right here."

LYDIE

The guard at the White House knew?

DAN

Yes! No. My first lie.

JOSHUA

You didn't go to the White House.

DAN

I stayed in the hotel room staring at the remaining letters "A.D.A.N." which quickly rearranged themselves into "N.A.D.A." "Nothing doing." If I ever showed up at the "Casa Blanca," I'd be left with "Nada."

I got on a train to New York with my very glad Gladstone bag. Spent a few days in a hotel in New York. Spent one bill on a fancy dinner. To risk if it were marked. I could always say I didn't know where the money came from. Waited. Waited. Kept looking behind me. No one's going to follow me. Nada. Nobody is looking for this money. Nobody wants to be caught looking for this money. This money has so many sharks swimming around it no one is going to risk sailing into these waters. I wired my son at his grandparents that I wanted him here. Wired the railroad. Said I had to be with my son. Family obligations. Quit my job. Got on a ferry this morning. I've been here a few hours. Wanted to enjoy it all. Being here. Savoring all of you. Feeling free for the first time. I swam out. I've been out there in the sea. Clean. Clean. Watching you from so far away. Seeing you. Loving you so much. And I thought this utopia's getting too *boor-goyse*. Married. Babies. Settling down.

LYDIE

What's that word?

DAN

Settling down?

JOSHUA

Boor-goyse?

DAN

French. You showed it to me in a book how the *boor-goyse* had
to be destroyed.

JOSHUA

Bourgeois. Bourgeois.

DAN

We believed we had been saved in the war to discover something
better. We can finally afford something better. Let Joshua publish his book if that's what he wants. I'm in a railroad uniform.
You in your nurse's uniform. We're all in the wrong uniform.
Look at me. Don't look away. Don't be like Dixie Land. Don't
look away, look away. The future is finally here. Utopia has to be
twenty-four hours a day. Or it doesn't count.
    (DAN *spills the money out of the bag.* LYDIE *and*
    JOSHUA *touch it.*)
Unmarked. Untraceable. Manna. Yes, that's what it is. Manna.
What a beautiful word. Manna. Manna.

JOSHUA *stands up, disturbed. He walks away from it.* LYDIE *holds the money.*

LYDIE

What we could do with this. We could build a paradise. My
god! This stack is the Orphanage. This handful is the Free
Clinic. This pile—

JOSHUA

To have money.

DAN

All our excuses taken away. We sit here and dream. We don't
like something, we have to change it. Our poverty is our excuse
for not doing anything. No more.

LYDIE

Show the workers the creation of a new world.

JOSHUA

We can create a new world!

They are thunderstruck by the enormity of this possibility. They look at the money with reverence.

LYDIE

Years from now, people will come here. This house will be a great museum. When did America turn around and start taking care of its people? Nantucket. Eighteen seventy-five. Yes, There were mills. We closed them down. Yes, it was a Herculean task, but we didn't question it. It didn't seem Herculean at the time. It was something that simply had to be done. I want to study Italian, Joshua. I want to read *The Divine Comedy* in the original. We've been through *The Inferno*. Let's be ready for *Paradiso*.

DAN

Freedom.

LYDIE

Freedom.

JOSHUA

Freedom.

They listen to the sea. A sound. A wagon? JOSHUA *stands at the top of the dune.*

JOSHUA

Dan, a police wagon just pulled up in front of the house.

LYDIE

It's the heart-attack man—the shot man!

DAN

No! It can't be.

They race to hide the money, scrap the bottles, the evidence of the feast.

LYDIE

Give them their money back! They traced the money!

JOSHUA

Say it was a mistake!

LYDIE

You haven't spent but a wee bit. We can make that up. Hide
the bottles. Bury the feast. Oh damn. Oh damn it all.

JOSHUA

Don't bury the damned bottles. Bury the bag.

DAN

We'll say we didn't know what it is.

AMOS *appears at the top of the dune, dressed in his Indian feathers and loin
cloth over his pants.*

AMOS

I got a ride out in the police wagon.

DAN, LYDIE, *and* JOSHUA *relax and roar with laughter.*

DAN

Oh, it's good.

LYDIE

See who's back?

AMOS

Hello, Dan. The police are fishing out at Tuckernuck.

DAN

Talk about the wrong uniform. Hee-chatta, ho-chatta.

AMOS

Stop laughing at me! Be quiet! Goddamit! Stop it! Cease!
        (*His sudden anger stops them cold.*)
You people have ruined me. I went to the Fete Day to meet
new people. I can't talk to anybody. I met the fishermen. All
they talked about was fish.

LYDIE

What did you expect them to talk about?

AMOS

And all I wondered about was what were you doing back here.
I forgot the fishing line in the ocean. Did Lydie remember to
change Gussie? Did you find the cow? I go away and Dan
comes back and you're all drunk and you're having a feast.

DAN

It's a going-away party.

JOSHUA

Belshazzar's Feast!

AMOS

Who's going away?

DAN

Shall we tell him?

LYDIE

You tell him.

JOSHUA

It's for you.

DAN

A going-away party for you.

JOSHUA & DAN

(*Sing softly*)
"For he's a jolly good fellow
For he's a jolly good fellow—"

AMOS

I'm not leaving. I went into town. I just came back.

DAN

Happy Going-Away.

AMOS

I live here. This is my home. I'm not leaving.

DAN

Some wine? Vou-vray!

AMOS

I went into town. You people have ruined me. I can only talk
to you. For better or for worse. I have to stay with you.

LYDIE

Be careful. That's what they say at weddings.

AMOS

Maybe I *am* married to all of you.

LYDIE

I'm spoken for.

JOSHUA

I'm taken, Amos.

AMOS

I mean this place. This backward Utopia. I come back to a going-away party. All backwards. All backwards. Aipotu.

JOSHUA

You could finally call this place The Oasis.

AMOS

I don't care what we call it.

JOSHUA

Or Arden.

DAN

Or Arcadia.

AMOS

I don't care. I'm home!

AMOS *puts his head in* LYDIE's *lap.*

JOSHUA

Because it could be an oasis. For you.

LYDIE

It seems you're going away to Harvard.

AMOS

Don't laugh at me.

DAN

How much money do you think it is?

JOSHUA

Oh, it's Harvard. I think they must charge a lot.

DAN *holds out a stack of bills.*

DAN

From us. To you.

DAN *puts the bills on* AMOS's *head.* AMOS *takes the money. He looks at it. He lets it drop. He stands.*

AMOS

You've shortened the sheet on my bed. You've put sawdust in my oatmeal. Put salt in my sugar bowl. Are we back to all of that?

AMOS *goes up to the house.*

JOSHUA

Amos!

DAN

He'll be back.

LYDIE

I'm going in the water. Give the remnants of this old gardenia plant a decent burial. Wash this day off me.

JOSHUA

Be careful.

LYDIE

Be careful? You tell *me* to be careful? *You* watch your daughter in her crib. *You* be careful.

JOSHUA

With Dan's money, we can buy forests of gardenias.

LYDIE *(Softly)*

Oh yes. Forests.

She picks up the gardenia and goes off to the sea. DAN *and* JOSHUA *watch her.*

DAN

She drops her blouse . . . that back . . . that most beautiful back . . . she undoes her skirt . . .

JOSHUA

Dan.

DAN

The aesthetic point of view. Like watching a painting. Or a great sculpture. In a museum in France. Or Germany. Or Italy. Don't you like museums?

They make a feint at boxing.

JOSHUA

I was going to ask you to get me a job on the railroad.

DAN

Joshua! You couldn't make it on the railroad.

JOSHUA

Does William Dean Howells control who gets hired on the railroad? "Not only do I reject that man's book, I will see to it that no railroad ever hires—"

DAN

You'd want to know the life story of every ticket you punched.

JOSHUA

I get involved in the details.

DAN

You're the fellow at the crossing waving a red flag as we gallop lickety larrup by. A human wave, waving as life speeds by. Look at Lydie Breeze swim out there. The way her arm lifts out of the water. See, Joshua, I can notice the detail too.

Pause.

JOSHUA

I've picked the wrong life. I'll have to change. Now I have the money. I can change.

DAN

You change? Mr. Darwin is not a magician demonstrating the impossible.

JOSHUA

What am I supposed to do? If this is me . . .

DAN

Keep writing and don't worry.

JOSHUA

Of course. The money solves everything.

DAN

It does. Those philosophers that Howells mentioned in his letter.

JOSHUA

Schopenhauer.

DAN

Had you heard of him?

JOSHUA

I've heard of everybody a little bit. I just don't know what to do with them.

DAN

Why don't you go to Europe to find out?

JOSHUA

Lydie wouldn't want to leave here. We have so much to do. Getting into the mills. That's a giant proposition. But going to Europe? No . . .

DAN

Do everything. Sail to Egypt. Travel up the Nile. Down the Nile.

JOSHUA

Traveling with a baby. Suppose we have another?

DAN

On to India. The Orient. Chugga. Chugga. Chugga.

JOSHUA

Suppose the baby becomes sick? You know how careful Lydie is.

DAN

Then let Lydie stay.

JOSHUA

Here by herself?

DAN

I'll be here with my son.

JOSHUA

Centaurs were half horse and half man. Dan Grady is the new breed. Half locomotive, half man. He calls out the station stops of the universe—Italy! Egypt! India!—while I travel there and he stays in Nantucket.

DAN

You're seeing the world. Two years. Three years. No time at all. Travel the seven seas. Is that how many there are? Find out. Then come back and free the world. First, free yourself.

JOSHUA

A beautiful German word for this. *Wanderjahre.*

DAN

Your wandering years. William Dean Howells will seem like the pond over by Gibb's cranberry bog. You'll have a whole new picture of the world. Look at the way your wife kicks her feet. A little white wake of foam. Her arms paddle over her head.

JOSHUA

I don't want you staying here with her.

DAN

I thought we were above all that.

JOSHUA *(Vehement)*

She's my wife.

DAN

She's an equal member of the community.

Pause. They look out to sea.

JOSHUA

She floats on her back. The moonlight on her breasts.

DAN

She drifts. She treads water.

JOSHUA

I wish there was a war. Oh, Christ, I miss the war. I wish hordes of Vikings right now would sail up out of that sea. I'd find a sword and chop them down and blood would flow. I wouldn't even mind being back at Cold Harbor.

DAN

Do you want me to kill William Dean Howells? I'll do that for you. I can pay someone to kill him.

JOSHUA

After I leave for Europe.

DAN

Oh yes. After. Or do you want me to offer him money? Perhaps we could pay him money to change his opinion of your book? Do you want me to do that?

JOSHUA

He wouldn't take money. Not William Dean Howells.

DAN

I can try.

JOSHUA

You must not even contact—my God. You would!

DAN

I'll do anything you want *after* you leave America. You're the captain. Sergeant Daniel Grady reporting to Captain Joshua Hickman.

Pause.

JOSHUA

Why is the sea so calm?

DAN

She's swimming underwater.

Pause.

JOSHUA

Lydie?

DAN

Lydie?

They run back and forth along the shore in a panic.

SCENE THREE

Dawn. LYDIE *is wrapped in a blanket. She holds the copy of "Bulfinch's Mythology" to her. The remnants of last night's feast—the pots and pans and bottles—are still scattered on the beach.* DAN *comes down from the house.*

DAN

Lydie, we're looking for you.

LYDIE

You men. Up all night drinking.

DAN

Lydie.

LYDIE

Red sky at morning. Sailors take warning. Last night. In the sea. That sea.

DAN

You almost drowned.

LYDIE

No. I was keeping my head up.

DAN *sits by her.*

DAN

Don't die on me just when we're beginning.

LYDIE

Oh no. Look the other way just in case any one's looking at us.

DAN

You haven't changed your mind? I won't have it, Lydie.

LYDIE

Dan, Dan, my darling Dan.

DAN

I won't have you changing your mind.

LYDIE

While I was swimming, it happened to me. Seeing the two of you talking on this shore. In this place. Or perhaps the money. Or perhaps just the relief of you home. Or perhaps. Perhaps.

DAN

The sea—so still.

LYDIE

Last night in the ocean, I blossomed. Like my gardenia in the old days. This blossom came out of me. Yes! All this blood rushed out of me and the ocean turned dark maroon around me and this perfectly formed *miniature* bobbed up to the surface for just a moment. And then the pain went away. And I tried to grab onto it, but the ocean took away the dark maroon and everything was clear again and I felt so clear and looking up at this shore seeing you there I felt so close to you.
    (Pause)
The child was yours. A child from you and me. A child from this place. I thought you'd never come back, and I'd never tell you we had conceived. I even had this horrid thought that you and I would never be able to conceive. That there'd never be a child from us. But we can. I saw it. It. It. What is the It?

DAN

The sea has this child, but the next one will be ours.

LYDIE

Feel the first of the sun.

DAN

Red sky in the morning.

LYDIE

Sailor take warning.

AMOS, *joyously drunk, comes to the top of the dune, carrying the wine and glasses. He dances.*

AMOS

I'm going to Harvard. I'm going to the law school. I know the history of Harvard. John Harvard found it. I forget the year, but it was back there and maybe Athens, Greece was as good, but Athens, Greece wasn't any better than Harvard College in

Cambridge, Massachusetts. And all the best people in the world go there and now I'm going to go there and I won't be too old and that's the story of Harvard, soon to include me! I forgot to give you the wine.

AMOS *slides down the dune, trying not to spill a drop of the wine.* DAN *takes two glasses and gives one to* LYDIE.

AMOS (very grand)

I'll pour.
>   (AMOS *pours them each a drop and keeps the rest*
>   *for himself.* AMOS *takes a handful of bills out of his*
>   *pocket.*)
Joshua found the most wonderful poem! I wrote it down on the money!
>   (*Reads on a series of bills:*)
"Be drunk.
Don't ever not be drunk.
If you don't want to feel time
Press down on you
And grind you
And crush you
Then you'd better stay drunk.
Always.
Drunk with what?
I don't care.
Poetry.
Goodness.
Even wine.
But be drunk."
Isn't that a great poem!

AMOS *leans over* LYDIE *and falls.*

LYDIE

Don't let him fall on me.

DAN

Be careful!

AMOS

Gussie. I'll wait for Gussie. Gussie Hickman, no fisherman's daughter for me. I'll wait for Gussie.

The sun has risen. JOSHUA *appears at the top of the dune. He wears the Indian headdress and the loincloth and carries the Gladstone bag.*

JOSHUA

You forgot the guest of honor!

AMOS

I'm the guest of honor.

JOSHUA

You left the guest of honor on the kitchen table.

JOSHUA *tosses the bag of money to DAN.*

DAN

Give it to me, you beauty. We'll buy up the whole damned island.

LYDIE

For the purpose—the sole purpose—of closing down the mills over on the mainland. Bring all the workers back here. We'll turn my father's house into a clinic. To heal them.

DAN

We'll turn Nantucket into a kingdom.

AMOS

An island kingdom.

DAN

An island kingdom owned by us!

JOSHUA

The perfect island kingdom! The revolution's begin—

JOSHUA *stops. A terrified* WOMAN *and a seven-year-old* BOY *appear at the top of the dune. Each carries a suitcase. The* BOY *has a tag on his lapel bearing his name and destination.*

JOSHUA

Dan.

DAN

Jeremiah? Beaty? I got the wrong date. Oh Christ. Oh Jesus Christ. You came on the morning ferry.

JOSHUA

Is there a coach up there?

BEATY

We need to pay him—

BEATY *speaks with a brogue.*

JOSHUA

Do we have money? Do we have money! Money!

JOSHUA *opens the Gladstone bag and bursts out laughing. He goes up the dunes and off as* JEREMIAH *and* BEATY *come down.* DAN *picks up* JEREMIAH *and holds him.*

JEREMIAH

Are you my father?

DAN

Jeremiah, I am your father. Everyone, this is my son and this is Beaty.

JEREMIAH

Is she my mother?

DAN

No.

JEREMIAH

Is my mother here?

DAN

She's not here.

JEREMIAH

I thought maybe my mother would be here.

DAN

Your mother died a long time ago.

JEREMIAH

My grandparents told me that, but I thought perhaps they did not know the truth.

DAN

They know the truth.

JEREMIAH

That lady right there?

DAN

She'll be like your mother. Lydie Breeze.

LYDIE

Hello, Jeremiah.

JOSHUA *returns.*

JOSHUA

You've come just in time for the revolution.

LYDIE

The new man.

DAN

Can you read?

JEREMIAH

No.

DAN

We'll teach you. Everyone, this is my son and this is Beaty. You're home.

LLYDIE *circles* BEATY, *sizing her up.*

LYDIE

What myth are you? We're going into the mills to free the workers. We need people who dream gigantic dreams.

BEATY

Myth? I don't know . . .

LYDIE

We have an opening for a Cassandra who can always see the future and no one believes her.

JOSHUA

I've been reading through this book and we definitely need a Cassandra.

BEATY

What is that book?

LYDIE

Bulfinch's Mythology! The World and its Origins. By Thomas
Bulfinch, native of Boston! All you need to know.

BEATY suddenly turns out to the audience, beaming. She steps forward:

BEATY *(to us)*

I must tell you the first day I saw them.

When I came to America, which would be a few years ago, I
stepped off the ship at Boston onto Rowe's Wharf and looked
up to see a golden dome. Did the immigrant ship transport me
to Jerusalem? I am in a holy place. I knelt down to worship.
"No," said the man who pulled me up and stamped my papers,
"you are in Boston and that is the state house designed by Mr.
Charles Bulfinch." I stared and stared at the golden dome.

I got my first job on Mount Vernon Street cleaning a beautiful house on a beautiful square. I heard the owners talking
one day talking to guests from England. "Who built this
house? Who built this square?" My employer said, "Mr.
Charles Bulfinch." I dropped the tray I carried. "Mr. Charles
Bulfinch?" They fired me.

Now another name I admired all over Boston was Nina.
Everywhere I went I saw written on walls Nina Nina. What a
popular girl. Should I change my name to Nina? I'd belong
here if my name was Nina. Then I learned Nina meant "No
Irish Need Apply."

I didn't know where to go. I couldn't get work. I couldn't go
back to Ireland. I couldn't stay in America. If I could only find
Mr. Bulfinch and serve him! Where is he? I wanted to die. I
got on a train. The conductor came to punch my ticket. I con-
fessed I didn't have a ticket—nor anything. No destination. He
looked at me till I turned red. "I know an island," he said. And
he gave me a job to claim his son and bring him here.

I arrived.

I saw these people in the sunlight, acting out gods and god-
desses. *Bulfinch's Mythology.* I took that book and I knew I
was home.

BEATY *steps back into the scene.*

LYDIE

I say it again. We need a Cassandra who sees the future.

BEATY

I see the future. Only happiness.

LYDIE

My kind of Cassandra.

JEREMIAH *points out to the sea.*

JEREMIAH

What's that called?

DAN

Where?

JEREMIAH

That watery part there.

DAN

The watery part? Kid, that's the Atlantic Ocean. The watery part? Kid, did you ever hear of Christopher Columbus?

JEREMIAH

No.

DAN

That's what he sailed. Did you ever hear of Magellan and Cortez and Sir Walter Raleigh and the Spanish Armada and the Mayflower. Can't forget the Mayflower! And every one of us had relatives that sailed across that watery part to get here.

JEREMIAH

What are those white flowery things on the watery part?

LYDIE

Where?

JEREMIAH

They look like parts of flowers.

LYDIE *looks out to sea.*

LYDIE

They do. They look like white petals.

JOSHUA

It's my manuscript. If you could throw your dead gardenia in
the sea, I reckoned I could heave in my manuscript—my
Prolegomena to Duty. Look at it finally bloom. Bye-bye.

JOSHUA *waves to his manuscript.*

LYDIE *(Aghast)*

Your book.

JOSHUA

Time to start all over again.

DAN

Yes! Start all over again. Jeremiah Grady, this is Lydie Breeze
Hickman.
 (JEREMIAH *shakes hands with* LYDIE.)
And this is Amos Mason, who's going off to Harvard.

AMOS *(Very grand)*

How do you do?

DAN

And this is Joshua Hickman.
 (JEREMIAH *and* JOSHUA *bow and shake hands.*)
We were all in the war together. We survived a war. We are
now very rich. These are my friends. Say good-bye to Joshua.
He's going on a trip back across the watery part.

AMOS

Jeremiah, get your shoes off.
 (AMOS *takes off the boy's boots.*)
You are about to be baptized in the greatest watery part of all
time!

LYDIE *(Disbelieving, to* JOSHUA*)*

You're going on a trip?

JOSHUA

I've made a great decision.

DAN

He's traveling first class.

LYDIE

Where?

JOSHUA

I want to see life firsthand. To see the real information. To see what I can bring back here. To learn.

LYDIE

You can't leave.

JOSHUA

Lydie, think of Thoreau writing *Walden*. Everybody is afraid to point out that Henry David Thoreau had pots of money. If money's good enough for Thoreau, money's good enough for Joshua. I earned it.

DAN

We all earned it! We are veterans!

JOSHUA

Lydie, I looked at a map of the world. My god, the Orient. The Nile. Egypt. Greece. I'll write everything down and bring it to you.

LYDIE

For how long?

JOSHUA

In terms of evolution, no time at all. A year.

DAN

It's good news, isn't it?

LYDIE

It's the wine talking. He hasn't decided anything.

DAN

Oh, he's decided.

JOSHUA

I'll finally see Europe.

LYDIE

You can't leave me. We are in this together.

DAN

Lydie. We can have everything we want.

LYDIE *angrily starts to heave the Gladstone bag in the sea.*

LYDIE

Take the money away. Take it back. Throw it in the sea!

DAN *and* AMOS *restrain her.*

DAN

No.

AMOS

No.

JEREMIAH

No!

JOSHUA *takes the bag from her.* LYDIE *walks away in a rage and sits, her back to them. An uncomfortable silence. Then:*

AMOS

Now in honor of the boy's first day here, I think we should seriously consider this performance of "Bulfinch." Mythology comes to Massachusetts, which we will perform as soon as I graduate from Harvard!

DAN

As soon as Joshua comes back from circling the world, we will go to Lowell, where greedy disciples of President Ulysses S. Grant have chained thousands of workers to giant machines spewing out cotton—

AMOS

How will we get in? I know! The old Trojan Horse routine!

DAN

Lydie will get us into the mills. She'll charm the mill owners. "Let us put on a play for your workers. You'll get more work out of them if they are properly entertained." Lydie gets us in. We're in the mills. We look up at the gigantic machines. There is silence.

JOSHUA, DAN, AMOS *in the moment look up at the enormity of the machines. They pick up pots and pans and begin beating them. They link arms and form a machine, making appropriate chugging and beating noises as they advance on* LYDIE.

JOSHUA

The Creation of the World, presented to you, the Workers of the World! *Bulfinch's Mythology. The World and its Origins.*

BEATY *proudly holds up the copy of* Bulfinch's Mythology.

AMOS

"Before earth and sea and heaven were created, all things wore one aspect to which we give the name Chaos—a confused shapeless mass."

JOSHUA *(To* JEREMIAH*)*

Say "God put an end to this discord."

JEREMIAH

"God put an end to this discord."

JEREMIAH *joins the machine.*

DAN

"Stars began to appear. Fishes took possession of the sea, birds of the air, and four footed beasts of the land."

JOSHUA

"A new creature was wanted!" Workers, that's what you are! We are offering you freedom!

AMOS

Workers of the world, listen to us and free yourselves. Unchain yourself from your machines.

LYDIE *relents. She stands. She kisses* JOSHUA. *She kisses* AMOS. *She kisses* DAN.

LYDIE

A new music. Yes! Keep the money. Go to the world. Go to Harvard. God gave us an upright stance so we can raise our eyes to heaven and gaze upon the stars. And what will we see?

JOSHUA

Freedom!

AMOS

Freedom!

DAN

Freedom!

LYDIE

Freedom.

JEREMIAH *picks up the money and hurls it overhead.*

JEREMIAH

Look at all this money!

Blackout

ACT TWO

SCENE ONE

A dank prison cell. A printing press. Stacks of paper. Cans of ink. A "guillotine"' which slices the paper into proper size. A cabinet containing type. Detritus of the print shop lies scattered about the floor. Pages hang off string stretched above the type cabinet. The only item betraying the whereabouts of this press is the barred window looking down into the courtyard of the Charlestown Prison, across the river from Boston, in the shadow of Bunker Hill.

It is nine years later, 1884. December. In the distance, the sound of hammers pounding nails. Morning drizzle. Gray light. AMOS MASON *is obviously a stranger to this room. The years have been kind to him, remarkably kind. He looks as if Sargent had painted Henry VIII in a beautifully cut gray suit. A chorus of children's voices singing a mournful hymn puzzles* AMOS *and makes him smile. But then a sudden and sharp scream in the courtyard takes away the smile.* O'MALLEY, *the Irish guard, unlocks the cell and comes into the room.*

O'MALLEY

May I get you a chair?

AMOS

That scream.

O'MALLEY

You can have a very fine view of the proceedings from here if you crook your neck around—

AMOS

I do not want to see the hanging. Nor sit. I only came to see Mr. Hickman and if he could hurry.

O'MALLEY

Oh dear. What impression can we be giving with all the clutter. On a normal day Mr. Hickman always cleans up everything ship-shape. But last night, with all the doings of today, Mr. Hickman was pressed onto the kitchen detail.

AMOS

I was told Mr. Hickman only worked here.

O'MALLEY

And those powers told you a truth. But the Brighton Mauler— the creature who's meeting his Maker today—now the Mauler worked on the kitchen detail and the kitchen-men, don't they start refusing to work as a tribute to their soon-to-be-deceased brother. Mr. Hickman has been pressed into his duties.

AMOS

Do you have to stand so close to me?

O'MALLEY

Sir, I had the choice of attending the hanging or escorting an honored guest. I chose you.

AMOS

If you'd like to go to the hanging, I release you.

O'MALLEY

I made a choice. I'll abide by my choice.

O'MALLEY *starts to sweep and tidy the room.*

AMOS

Are those children singing?

O'MALLEY

They're not prisoners. They're the children of the prison master and the keeper and the sheriff all come up for today's festivities.

AMOS

Festivities?

O'MALLEY

Aye, festivities. Every greenhorn in Boston will be dancing tonight. The Brighton Mauler would prey on immigrants newly settled in Boston and he'd garrotte them and pluck the gold out of their teeth and hurl their bodies back in the ocean they'd just crossed.

AMOS

They don't keep Joshua—Mr. Hickman—anywhere near the likes of the Brighton Mauler?

O'MALLEY

Just to inform you. When the wife of the Brighton Mauler came up yesterday to say her last goodbyes and she learned your friend was here, she screamed out, "You don't have my husband locked up with the likes of that devil from Nantucket!"

AMOS

Joshua Hickman is no devil.

AMOS *lifts a page off the drying string.*

O'MALLEY

Mr. Hickman don't like no one meddling with his work.

AMOS *(Reads:)*

"Wait and hope."

O'MALLEY

"The Count of Monte Cristo."

AMOS

Is it good to have this kind of literature in prison?

O'MALLEY

It's how Mr. Hickman teaches the men to read.

AMOS

Famous escapes?

O'MALLEY

It's all the men are interested in, no matter what side of the bars we're on. We move our fingers word by word over the prison scenes in "Les Misérables" and we go over the parts of the Bible where the angel leads the men out of prison. Now take me, for an instance. Your friend is more than just a convicted murderer to me. He is my teacher. Four years ago I was an illiterate donkey. Today I can pick up a book and read it from top to bottom, whether it has prison escapes in it or no.

AMOS

Mr. Hickman still has his knack of instilling people with ideals.

O'MALLEY

Sir, all I want is for Joshua Hickman to get what he deserves.

AMOS

That's all I want.

O'MALLEY

I've done the right thing.

AMOS

Oh, yes.

O'MALLEY

I'm very pleased and elated to meet you.

JOSHUA *enters, a jacket over his striped prison uniform. He looks remarkably fit. His hands are stained with ink.*

AMOS

Joshua.

JOSHUA

Amos.

AMOS

Are you all right?

JOSHUA

Yes.

AMOS

That hammering.

JOSHUA

I like a day like this. The food is always better when they have a hanging. They feed us to keep us calm.

AMOS

It's glorious to see you.

JOSHUA

I requested not to see you. My objection was overruled.

O'MALLEY

Sir, he's traveled a ways to be here.

JOSHUA *looks at* AMOS, *then goes to the press.*

JOSHUA

O'Malley, did you hear the scream?

AMOS

I came up from New York especially.

JOSHUA *(Ignoring* AMOS*)*

The priest came by to give the condemned man a fair shake at heaven.

AMOS

Joshua, listen to me.

JOSHUA

The priest put out the crucifix for the Brighton Mauler to kiss and the Brighton Mauler bit the head off the gold crucifix and spat the head of Christ right in the face of the chaplain.

AMOS

Joshua—

O'MALLEY

Excuse me one second. The Mauler bit the head off Christ?

JOSHUA

He broke his teeth off in the bargain.

O'MALLEY

Those were the screams?

JOSHUA

"What do I mind the pain for? Get this hanging over."

O'MALLEY

Mr. Mason, would you allow me to take leave of my assignment just for a moment?

AMOS

Of course.

JOSHUA

O'Malley, don't leave me alone with him.

O'MALLEY

I think you'll be perfectly safe. Earlier today, this had given the outward appearances of being a much more straightforward execution. The head of Christ! Mother of Jesus.

O'MALLEY *is gone. The sound of the bolt locking echoes.* JOSHUA *works at the press.*

AMOS

The Brighton Mauler.

JOSHUA

In some ways, he was a good man.

AMOS

You don't seem upset.

JOSHUA

We've known for a long time he was going to die. On this day. We're not surprised. I taught him to read. He called down the corridor last night: "Mr. Hickman, how does *Robinson Crusoe* end?" I called back: "He goes home." The Mauler: "Sir, is that a happy ending?" "Yes," I called back.
     (Pause.)
Have you seen Lydie?

AMOS

Not in so many words.

JOSHUA

You don't see someone with words. You see them or you don't.

AMOS

I'm in touch with her.

JOSHUA

One sense more than I am.

Pause.

AMOS

I had imagined you more—

JOSHUA

What?

AMOS

Broken.

JOSHUA

I'm very happy here. You mustn't be upset for me.

JOSHUA *goes to the type cabinet.*

I don't even have to look anymore. I hold up the type stick and
pluck the letters in and out of the case . . . I can compose right
on the press. I have become a machine. And I have to keep my
head well oiled because I must set page one with page thirty-
two. Page two with page thirty-one. I've learned to guillotine
the pages down to the proper size. Sew them into a book. I
couldn't even sew a button on. Now I'm a printer and a
teacher. That Brighton Mauler read a whole chapter from
"The Count of Monte Cristo" before his time came up. It was
a real triumph. Be careful of that ink on your suit.
    (AMOS *moves away quickly.*)
It's a beautiful suit. The world must love you to give you that
suit for a uniform.

AMOS

I'm frankly quite sick to my stomach being here today.

JOSHUA *takes a bun out of his handkerchief and begins eating.*

JOSHUA *(Cheery)*
Would you like a bun?

AMOS
My wife is waiting for me at the hotel.

JOSHUA
Old Amos is married? Bravo!

AMOS
My partner's daughter.

JOSHUA
Partner?

AMOS
In my law firm.

JOSHUA
Law firm?

AMOS
My law firm. Wharton Commager.

JOSHUA
Hallelujah! You *are* catching brass rings! Could I print you some business cards?

AMOS
I have sufficient, thank you.

JOSHUA
You've been fishing?

AMOS
Not fishing. Sufficient.

JOSHUA
I always see you fishing. Forgetting to take your line in. I could print you up a very attractive letterhead.

AMOS

Our firm has its stationery needs quite under control

JOSHUA

If I need a lawyer—

AMOS

We're finance.

JOSHUA

Boston?

AMOS

New York.

JOSHUA

How is New York?

AMOS

Fine. Talking about you only the other day.

JOSHUA

I'm sure I'm on everybody's lips. How do you spell *recommend*? It's one of those words I can never—

AMOS

I saw William Dean Howells.
        (Pause.)
He's read your new book.
        (Pause.)
The book you wrote here.

JOSHUA

The book?

AMOS

Your book. *Aipotu: A Nantucket Memory.*

JOSHUA

No one knows about my book. I printed up five copies of my book. For my personal use. Not to be sent—

JOSHUA *pulls out a box from under the press.*

One. Two. Three. Four.

He takes out four hand-bound volumes.

Where is the fifth copy?

O'MALLEY *unbolts the door and runs in.*

> O'MALLEY
> Sir, you're not watching out the window! Sir, you'll see a mirac-
> ulous accident! They hauled the Brighton Mauler up on the
> gallows!

> JOSHUA
> What have you done with my book?

> O'MALLEY *(To* AMOS*)*
> You told him?

> AMOS
> Mr. O'Malley sent a copy of your book to Mister Howells in
> New York.

> JOSHUA
> When?

> O'MALLEY
> Last month. You were in the infirmary with the influenza.

> JOSHUA
> What have you done to me? This man—this Howells—wants
> me dead. What kind of betrayal—

JOSHUA *grabs* O'MALLEY. AMOS *separates them.*

Where is the fifth copy?

> AMOS
> I have it here.

AMOS *produces the fifth copy of the hand-bound book.* JOSHUA *takes it.*

> JOSHUA
> That book does not leave here. You sent a copy to Howells?
> Are you mad? O'Malley?

> O'MALLEY
> Sir, don't be angry with me!

AMOS

Read this letter.

O'MALLEY

There's a letter, Sir.

AMOS *hands* JOSHUA *a letter.* AMOS *does not take his eyes off* JOSHUA *as* JOSHUA *reads the letter.* O'MALLEY *gives* AMOS *the full dirt:*

They brought the Mauler up on the gallows. The beam holding the rope cracked with the weight of the Mauler and the Brighton Mauler falls down in the snow and the black bag is half off his head and the blood pouring out from his mouth where he bit off the cross. "Is this death?" He's back in his cell now screaming in pain while they mend the gallows and fix his teeth.

Pause.

JOSHUA *(Reads:)*

"The soul of a nation is in literature. These pages you send me from the Charlestown prison—"

AMOS

He starts out "Dear Colleague."

JOSHUA

Is this letter true?

AMOS

It's quite real. I just got it. I wanted you to see it. Wouldn't even trust it to the mails.

JOSHUA

"The pages you send me . . . The fragments . . . Suggest a way to the American literature I am trying to create . . ." Am I truly reading this?

AMOS

Oh yes.

O'MALLEY *proudly reads over* JOSHUA's *shoulder:*

O'MALLEY

"Fragments of memory movingly detail . . . America after . . . The tragic War Between the States . . . Three soldiers come to an island to create an ideal—"

AMOS
You don't have to tell me the plot. I am the plot.

JOSHUA *(To* O'MALLEY*)*
The Mauler's still alive?

O'MALLEY
Yes, sir. Still alive! You can hear—

JOSHUA
I'd love to show him the letter.

O'MALLEY
Couldn't you print it up in the bulletin? Let everyone see it—

A bell rings in the room. O'MALLEY *responds. To* AMOS.

I'm locking you in, sir. But should there be any emergency, any
emergency at all, you ring that bell.

AMOS
We'll be fine. I'm sure.

O'MALLEY *goes. The sound of the bolt echoes.*

JOSHUA
He wants to work with me on the book. He'll come to Boston.
He says I have the raw material—I'm dizzy, Amos. Look.

AMOS
Yes. Quite a difference from nine years ago.

JOSHUA *(Reads:)*
"Your uncanny selection of details creates a haunting—"

AMOS
You let Howells off lightly with your uncanny omission of the
way he treated you. The other manuscript—the *Prolegomena*.
The rejection. You just blithely pass over—

JOSHUA
Oh, Amos, that was too painful to write about.

AMOS
But you write so vividly about killing Dan Grady.

JOSHUA

That was easy to write. I picked up the horseshoe. I beat Dan's head in. I described it.

Pause.

AMOS

Howells came up to me in the Harvard Club. He gave me this book. Had I ever heard of a horseshoe murder on Nantucket? Howells says, "Are you part of all this? Stolen money?" Howells wanted to know all about the stolen money. Hoax. I told him it was a hoax.

JOSHUA

The book is no hoax.

AMOS

I said I'd have to take it home and read it. Which I did. Quite shocking. To go to the Harvard Club for a drink. For a round of billiards. Not for an hallucination. To be handed this book. Set in type. *A fait accompli.* There's my name. There I am. There's Dan. There's Lydie. I came to Boston.

JOSHUA

And? And?

AMOS

And what?

JOSHUA

Did Howells say?

AMOS

I told him I was coming to see you. I told Howells you were very damaged. It would be best if I played the middleman. He gave me the letter.

JOSHUA

You read the book?

AMOS

Oh yes.

JOSHUA

God, this is like going to the dentist! Did you like it?

AMOS

The book? I don't understand its purpose.

JOSHUA

Purpose?

AMOS

Why do you say we were Socialist?

JOSHUA

We were Socialist.

AMOS

Why do you talk about Dan Grady stealing the money?

JOSHUA

Dan Grady stole the money.

AMOS

Why do you locate me at the murder scene?

JOSHUA

You were at the murder scene.

AMOS

Because I was there that day is precisely why you must not let
this book go any further.

JOSHUA

Are you mad?

AMOS

I don't want you publishing this book.

JOSHUA

Amos. I never sought publication.

AMOS

So you don't think anything of the book.

JOSHUA

I had done it for other reasons. But this changes everything.

AMOS

It changes nothing.

JOSHUA

Oh. You hate being caught off-guard there in the Harvard
Club. I should've written you. Begged your permission. Pled
your imprimatur. Mr. Mason of the New York law firm, allow
me to tell the story of my life.

AMOS

The book will not be published.
    (Pause.)
In a way, I come here representing not just myself but, more
importantly, the interests of a man who cannot defend himself.

JOSHUA

Who the devil is that?

AMOS

Because Dan Grady is a member of our largest majority. The
dead. What would Dan think of these pages? His death
bandied about.

JOSHUA

Amos.

AMOS

Just because one is dead doesn't mean he forfeits his rights.

JOSHUA

Oh, you are a lawyer.

AMOS

If I didn't want you to have this letter, I could have stopped it
as easily as winking. Simply withheld the letter. Or told
Howells you were a lunatic. Or answered Howells in your
name, that you wanted nothing of publication. Or paid off the
prison. I could find a myriad of ways to block your receiving
this letter. But you are my friend and I want you to have the
triumph and the pleasure of seeing Howell's response.

JOSHUA

Thank you.

AMOS

And that must be the end of it. Publication brings up much larger consequences. Think of all the friends this book would kill.

JOSHUA

Friends! Where have you been the last four years, my friend?

AMOS

I get reports on your well-being. You're not abandoned. When you killed Dan, you became like those men in the army who decided to help the enemy. I realized if I ever wanted a public life, I would have to treat you in the same way—strike you from the ranks.

JOSHUA

Then coming here today was a vast act of courage.

AMOS

I haven't found it easy denying you, Joshua.

JOSHUA

But you've kept trying.

AMOS

You are my friend. Three years ago I wrote the prison. What does he need? A printing press.

JOSHUA

You sent the press here?

AMOS

Gladly. I want the best for you. You taught me to recognize the best.

Pause.

JOSHUA

Howells wants me to publish my book.

AMOS

And you must not let him.

JOSHUA

Ohhhhh, I see. I smell politics. Fee-fi-fo-fum. You want to go into politics.

AMOS

Yes.

JOSHUA

My book becomes an inconvenience.

AMOS

Yes.

JOSHUA

Congress?

AMOS

Senate.

JOSHUA

Massachusetts?

AMOS

New York.

JOSHUA

And you've developed all these lovely cogs and spokes and hooks and facets so it's easier for the machinery to pick you up. And my book dents and tarnishes your rise to glory.

AMOS

Not my rise to glory. What will this book do to your daughters? All their lives pursued by this ruthless shadow. Their father a murderer. Is that any kind of dowry? Fathers should give their daughters at the least an emotional dowry. And Jeremiah, Dan's boy, sent off to England. What about him? And Lydie— you have Lydie getting in and out of beds. My God, the nature of time—the very essence of time—is to heal. And in this timeless place you deny time its purpose. You only rip open wounds. Hurl mud on your wife. Brand your children.

JOSHUA

And if I don't publish the book?

AMOS

Howells is offering you publication. I'm offering you freedom.

JOSHUA

Freedom?

AMOS

A pardon. Full. Complete. I have an appointment with Governor Butler at five today. I explained everything to him. How you killed Dan. Why you killed Dan. "My my" he said. "That's aggravated homicide. That's not second degree homicide to my way of thinking." Now no matter what we feel about Governor Butler's presidential aspirations, he is a very fair man. He'll give you a pardon. He'd like to. Christmas coming up. Everyone's heart swells. The whole world is Bethlehem.

JOSHUA

And what's the price of a room in Bethlehem these days?

AMOS

Ten thousand dollars.

JOSHUA

Where do we get ten thousand dollars?

AMOS

It's the last of Dan's money. I've invested it. Invested it well. I'd love to close out that account.

JOSHUA

And use it to buy my pardon for having killed Dan.

AMOS

Now that's irony, Joshua. That's irony. See? I'm learning. I've learned.

JOSHUA

You don't understand. I'm very happy here. Not just today with this letter. I always knew I'd get this letter. I saw the moment precisely. My first night in Europe. My ship had landed in Piraeus. I took the ferry over to Athens. Bought wine. Walked up to the Acropolis. I touched the Parthenon. The ground was still reeling under me from so many weeks at sea. The moon began to rise. They'd erected gates to keep out scavengers. I was locked inside the Parthenon. And at that moment—I swear to you—like some Delphic Oracle—I saw this moment. I saw this letter. William Dean Howells would change his mind. I knew that. And I pulled off my clothes and I recited all the Greeks and danced around the columns. I knew this letter would come. That I could write a book that would be the best of me. I've seen this moment. I am not only Dan's killer. His death is not my sum and total. This book. These pages. I saw this letter.

Pause.

AMOS

How do I summon the turnkey?

JOSHUA

He'll hear that bell.

AMOS *rings the bell.*

AMOS

You won't help me.

JOSHUA

No.

JOSHUA *goes to the press and begins setting type.*

In England, in small towns, printing shops still have medieval signs hanging outside. Two inkballs held by a dragon, snorting angry steam out of his nostrils. Thank you for this machine. It's the right machine for me.

O'MALLEY *unbolts the door and enters.*

AMOS

Fetch her.

O'MALLEY

He brought the lady. Sir, I did everything for the good. Sir?

O'MALLEY *goes.*

JOSHUA

Is Lydie here?

AMOS

She rode up with me in the carriage.

JOSHUA

You said you hadn't seen her.

AMOS

She was hoping not to see you.

JOSHUA

Lydie—Did you go to Nantucket?

AMOS

She's not allowed on Nantucket. Which is a tragedy. I can't think of Nantucket without seeing Lydie there. It was part of the judge's decision.

JOSHUA

Judge's decision?

AMOS

Leaving the island forever. All I know is last year Beaty heard these screams and ran in and saw Lydie Breeze over the pillow pushing down onto Gussie. Young Lydie had been locked away in the attic, apparently awaiting her turn. Lydie Breeze was going to kill both the children, but they were rescued. Thanks to Beaty passing by. They'll be put up for— Well, in foster homes . . .

Silence.

JOSHUA

I knew about it. O'Malley told me about it last year. I didn't know that Lydie Breeze was barred from the island. I thought she was still there. I thought.

AMOS

And you didn't do anything?

JOSHUA

I am here! They are there! I thought they were all together. I thought.

The door opens. O'MALLEY *leads* LYDIE *in. She looks inflamed. She is dressed in an elegant coat and hat which are too large for her. She is very thin.* JOSHUA *tries to touch her. She pulls away.*

JOSHUA

You're burning.

O'MALLEY

I wasn't told she had an influenza. We've had enough influenzas infecting the prison.

LYDIE

Don't worry. I won't pollute your prison.

Her voice is husky. Her teeth are dark.

JOSHUA

You haven't been nursing?

LYDIE

No, I haven't done that since— Oh, that time years ago.

JOSHUA

You know how it upsets you.

LYDIE

Why I became a nurse—what I imagined nursing to be—I can't remember that.

AMOS

Healing. You wanted to heal every broken thing.

LYDIE

Is that what it was? Perhaps. Yes.

JOSHUA

I've written a book about all of us.

LYDIE

So it seems!

JOSHUA

Did you—?

LYDIE

I opened it. Saw names. Moving up. Floating up. Dan. Lydie. That's me? In a book? Printed out? I wrapped it up. Mailed it back.

JOSHUA

He wants me to do something.

LYDIE

I know.

JOSHUA

Amos says it will destroy him.

LYDIE

Will it?

AMOS

Yes. I think so.

LYDIE

There you are.

JOSHUA

I hadn't thought.

LYDIE

Not thinking. That's what got us into trouble in the first place. We wanted perfection. So we assumed we were perfection. Thank god the girls are spared all of us.

JOSHUA

The girls?

LYDIE

Gussie's wonderful. Full of life. She has sides of you. After little Lydie begins reading and writing, I might like her more. It's hard to know what to expect from anyone named after me.

AMOS

She hasn't seen them in over a year, Joshua.

LYDIE

Amos, you tell all my secrets. You're like Joshua's book. Make everything public. This hanging going on. It's not yours? Is it? I thought Amos had arranged a wonderful surprise for me. But, no—one more disappointment.

AMOS

I'll leave you.

LYDIE

Yes. Yes. Please.

AMOS

Then you'll come back to the hotel?

LYDIE

Of course.

AMOS

My wife wants you to join us at tea.

LYDIE

I look forward to that.

AMOS

Joshua—

LYDIE

Please leave us.

AMOS *and* O'MALLEY *go. The sound of the locking bolt echoes.*

JOSHUA

Amos brought you here to convince me?

LYDIE

I don't see myself as a siren luring you.

JOSHUA

Let me hold you? Lydie, look at you. You in this room.

She turns from him.

LYDIE

This coat. It belongs to Amos's wife. This hat. I went to their
hotel. Had a bath. Amos's wife is very comfortable. Like a great
sofa. They dressed me. It seemed a matter of great import to
her how I looked.

*She takes off the coat and hat. Her dress is iridescent green, it is so black
and thin and worn. She looks around the room, examining the press.*

JOSHUA

Where are the girls?

LYDIE

They're on Nantucket. Beaty is looking after them. She writes to me. I can't read her letters. But the handwriting doesn't appear desperate, so I assume everything is . . . I've been here. In Boston. I live off Scollay Square. And then I go to Cambridge for three days. Not full time. But perhaps—

JOSHUA

Cambridge?

LYDIE

Yes. Amos and I finally have something in common. I'm at Harvard!

JOSHUA

Lydie.

LYDIE

As a char. I clean the rooms, the undergraduates. They have quite the parties and on Mondays they need extra girls to clean. It's like a little commune, college.

JOSHUA

I don't want you cleaning. Do you need money? Money was kept for the girls. For you. You still have the house?

LYDIE

The city is very exhilarating. Most times I walk from Scollay Square over Beacon Hill across the river into Cambridge. And the air is good. If the girls are put in homes, I hope it will be in Boston.

JOSHUA

I don't want the girls off the island. I want them growing up there. That is their home.

LYDIE

You don't know about the sand. It's like glass. The sand that's come coats the furniture, the beaches, the walls, our lungs. I'm afraid it's ripping us apart from the inside. If I don't look well, I am still suffering from the sand.

JOSHUA

Lydie, look at me.

LYDIE

The sand tastes of blood and smells of sulphur. There was a volcano that exploded on the other side of the world a year ago. August. Krakatoa? Well, this volcano erupted and sent this cloud over Africa and Asia and Europe and it picks up force and the volcanic dust has teeth in it and it sends down red rain. You haven't seen anything till you stick your head out of the window in the morning trying to get the children off to school and you see red rain streaming down. The sand red. The sea red. And the white church towers in Nantucket Town are red. The girls were so frightened. How was I going to protect them?

JOSHUA

Did you see Doctor Paynter?

LYDIE

Of course! I made an appointment because the girls were so scared, and Doctor Paynter explained to us very carefully, with red rain streaming down the panes of his office, that the winds from the volcano on the other side of the world caused these whirlwinds that rode over the land and scooped up herds of cattle—prides of lions—and took them into the sky and the volcanic dust ground them to bits and the red rain was only the blood of animals. The girls were so frightened. You know how children are? "Suppose we're taken into the air?" And Doctor Paynter laughed and I laughed. "That can't happen." And on the way home, I thought about Dan dying. We walked through the red rain. And I thought about you killing. And we stepped into great red puddles. And I said to the girls, "I will now give you a great lesson." Because the girls must be taught. "Anything can happen." That is the most horrid fact about living. Anything can happen. And we were home. And I looked at the house. And I looked at the red ocean. And it all had happened here. What we had been. What we had become. What we were. Dan Grady dead. Anything can happen. And I walked up the steps of the porch very carefully so the wind couldn't take me up. Or the girls. And I decided to protect the girls in the only way I knew.

The door is unbolted. AMOS *returns.*

JOSHUA

Right now for the first time. This is prison.

AMOS

I can see the Governor at five. The money can be transferred to his private account tomorrow. Two or three days. Papers signed. Review boards. Then Lydie appears before the judge and explains the change in her position.

LYDIE

What change in my position?

AMOS

Your husband is freed. Resumption of the family. A woman no longer alone.

LYDIE

But I *am* alone.

AMOS

The ship has regained its rudder. The two of you returned home.

LYDIE

You told me I could return to Nantucket to my children.

AMOS

And that is what will happen.

LYDIE

I could go back alone.

AMOS

The judge in Boston will not let you return to the island alone.

LYDIE

Your wife sat by the edge of my bath and rubbed my back and said, "Listen to Amos. This is the only way to get your children back." You told me if he agreed not to publish the book. You told me. I'm not going back to Nantucket with him. I'm not starting anything over. I want to be back with my children. That is all.

AMOS

The judge will not allow it, you by yourself with them.

LYDIE

Oh, you've worked it out with such finesse! But why do you only feel threatened by Joshua's revelations? I find it amazing how you trust me not to reveal anything from my side. I know about stolen money. I know about murder.

AMOS

I do trust you. Not to betray the past.

LYDIE

Joshua and I are not finished yet.

The door is unbolted. AMOS *leaves. The door is bolted.*

Oh, I could tell secrets. I know some secrets. Not as low as the secrets you reveal, of course, in your book.

JOSHUA

I revealed no secrets.

LYDIE

Is it true what you say about the gardenia?

JOSHUA

Yes. It's true.

LYDIE

You meant to destroy it.

JOSHUA

You were away. The letter of rejection came. I wanted to hurt something. Inflict a wound. Power over something. The book was rejected. You were away. There was this healthy blooming thing that you loved.

LYDIE

If I'd known that fact, Dan Grady would be alive today. I would have left you. I would not have stayed in a house with a murderer.

JOSHUA

I wanted to tell the truth.

LYDIE

But you didn't find the truth. I chose you. Hundreds of men in
that hospital and I chose you. I chose Dan. I chose Amos. The
truth is nowhere in your work. I stole medicine for you three and
I gave you special time and I said I will choose three men and I
will make a future out of them. Giants striding against the sky.

JOSHUA

We told ourselves we were giants far too long.

LYDIE

Eagles. Eagles doing battle.

JOSHUA

I wanted to reduce all the events of our life together to the size
of a photograph so that I could comprehend it and look at it
and—

LYDIE

Oh, a little Matthew Brady of the soul. You did that all right.
You did that. Your book is like a series of tiny photographs. No
nobility. No size. Not even Dan's death. You've read Poe.
Couldn't you have described Dan's death in a more fantastical
style?

JOSHUA

There was no noble motive. There was no great passion. The
same petty furies that made me kill the gardenia, those same
petty furies made me kill Dan. Rage over losing you. Oh,
Christ—in all our dreaming we never allowed for the squalid,
petty furies. We lived on a beach in a vast landscape. We mis-
took the size of the ocean, the size of the sky, for the size of our
souls. We were this great transparent eyeball trying to look into
the mind of God. It's taken this prison to show me our true
horizons. I want to look our petty furies in the face and name
them and lose them.

LYDIE

You went to Europe. To find your gods. You should've stayed

there until you found them. You are empty. You should've stayed in Europe. You never should have come back.

JOSHUA

Lydie, my one night in Europe, my one famous night, I stood in the Parthenon waiting for the connection with the ages to wash over me. I am ready for the ancient awe. Overhead, Athena and Zeus are trying to catch my attention. Sappho and Sophocles are about to sing their song. Yes! Plato and Aristotle are walking this very ground. It's dark. A slender moon. I wait. And all I saw was you. You were my voyage. You were my Europe. You were my mythology. The Parthenon became your temple. I lit candles. I kneeled at your feet. I danced to you. Shepherds rang bells far away. Goats bleated in the dark. I made up ancient rhythms and beat the columns and pounded my fists: Lydie! Lydie! Lydie! Lydie! Was I mad? Was I drunk? I heard your voice say very quietly: I know an island. And Plato and Sappho and Socrates say "Listen to that voice. Leave us all behind." And I picked up my gear and ran down the hills. And I called out. Lydeeeeeeeee. I'm sailing home.
    (Pause.)
You know the rest.

LYDIE

Your vision's complete. You have your book.

JOSHUA

It's all because of you.

LYDIE

Me?

JOSHUA

Because of your leg, really.

LYDIE

My leg?

JOSHUA

At night my brain used to start galloping lickety-larrup like one of Dan's railroads from earth to the moon, then down to the center of the earth. All my ideas and dreams and plans and quests and theories, and I'd wake up sweating and screaming. But one night you put your leg over on me. Just threw it over, tossed your leg over on me across my thighs. You just threw your leg out and left it there, and I didn't move because I didn't want to wake you and it pinned me down.

LYDIE

Trapped?

JOSHUA

No, the opposite. It was like the string on a balloon. You connected me and I could dream—go anywhere I wanted and never lose myself because I was connected to the earth. By this. By your gravity. I miss the feel of this leg on me. The heat between us. I could burn all the dross out of us. Leave only gold.

LYDIE

Well, that gold mine is closed. But I close my eyes. I see you all coming up the beach. I have enough pictures in my head to release some whenever I feel trapped. When my head gallops. Lickety-larrup. Like Dan Grady's railroads.

JOSHUA

You loved him.

LYDIE

Oh, yes. Never felt trapped when Dan was around.

JOSHUA

Did you love me?

Pause.

LYDIE

We were all part of the same passion.

JOSHUA

The first night we came to the island. You and I. The others hadn't arrived yet. We stepped off the ferry onto Nantucket, and we saw the captain of the ferry holding a yellow cage with two fierce red parrots, and then we saw two cattle being led off, and there was a rooster and there was a hen and a crew man led off two goats, and we realized we were the only two human passengers. And we began laughing.

LYDIE

After you, Mr. Noah.

JOSHUA

After you, Mrs. Noah . . .

LYDIE

And the two Noahs stepped off the Ark. And when we got to our house, I thought the earth would break open. The sand stuck to our skins and our skins wanted the sand and each other and the stars were fighting to break out of the sky and get down to us and you and I were leaping up to catch them. The war was over. This passionate attraction of everything on this planet for everything and everyone else. This caring, respect, extraordinary interest. Aipotu.

AMOS *enters, unobserved.*

Well . . . We were young.

Pause.

The hell with it. Publish your book.

JOSHUA

But the girls—

AMOS

Lydie!

LYDIE

They're strong. They're young.

JOSHUA

You?

AMOS

Lydie, we struck a bargain.

LYDIE *(To* JOSHUA*)*

Do what Howells tells you.

AMOS

You said you wanted your girls back. I thought I found a way
that made all of us happy.

JOSHUA *(To* LYDIE*)*

It can never be the book you want.

LYDIE

Eagles? Giants?

LYDIE *looks at him. He turns away.* O'MALLEY *runs in, breathless.*

O'MALLEY

The Mauler's unconscious! They're trying to revive the bugger!
We were all passing the whiskey around and the Mauler takes
advantage and he attacks two of the guards, Brody and
Brennan, and he leaps out the window, and he becomes this
devil possessed with demons, and he scales the walls and gets
to the very top and throws his head back: "The world is mine!"
Mr. Hickman, your very own words from *The Count of Monte
Cristo*! And then don't the Mauler lose his balance and fall off
the wall, back into the prison. The doctors are hovering over
him now because you ain't allowed to hang an unconscious
human.

LYDIE *has slipped out the door.*

JOSHUA

Lydie!

AMOS

Let her go.

JOSHUA

I want her.

JOSHUA *tries to pursue her.*

AMOS

Let her go!

O'MALLEY

Mr. Hickman!

JOSHUA

Lydie!

O'MALLEY

Joshua!

JOSHUA

Lydie, where will you go?

O'MALLEY

You're not allowed out there, Mr. Hickman!
>   (O'MALLEY *takes his truncheon and strikes* JOSHUA
>   *on the head.* JOSHUA *falls. To* AMOS:)
Will you be coming, sir?

AMOS

A moment.

O'MALLEY

I'll see the lady down to the entrance door. I'll be back for you.

O'MALLEY *goes.*

AMOS

Do you need a doctor?

JOSHUA

No . . .

AMOS

I assumed Lydie would plead my case.

JOSHUA

Miscalculation.

AMOS

She's hardly the one to make rational choices. My wife was
alarmed meeting Lydie. She—
>   (*Clapping begins in the distance. One–two–
>   three–four. One–two–three–four.* AMOS *goes to the
>   window.*)
What's that?

JOSHUA
The men. The prisoners. Us. Beginning to drum their tribute.

JOSHUA *goes to the press. He begins setting type on the chase. The sounds of the execution drown out the clapping. Suddenly, there is a scream and then silence.* JOSHUA *stops.* AMOS *looks away from the window.*

AMOS
Lydie needs her friends. My wife and I are so busy. We're in New York. Gertrude and I—our lives take up so much time.

JOSHUA
You want me to destroy the book?

AMOS
It would be loyal.

AMOS *looks at* JOSHUA *who gives no response.* AMOS *gives up and starts to go.*

Then JOSHUA *takes up the first volume of his book.* JOSHUA *places it in the guillotine and shreds it.* AMOS *watches.* O'MALLEY *returns and sees what's happening.* O'MALLEY *moves forward.* AMOS *stops* O'MALLEY.

JOSHUA *takes the second volume.* JOSHUA *examines the book. He touches the pages.* JOSHUA *places that volume in the guillotine.* JOSHUA *raises and lowers the blade on the pages. He takes the third volume . . .*

Curtain

Part II
The Sacredness of
the Next Task

ACT ONE

PROLOGUE

LYDIE BREEZE, *radiant, beautiful, appears out of the darkness, wearing a white dress, carrying a lantern and a book. She smiles, sits at a table, and opens the book.*

LYDIE BREEZE *(to us)*

The idea of freedom comes naturally to me. Read my father's logs. He was the captain of a whaling ship, *The Gardenia*. He took his wife with him. Listen: "The twenty-ninth day of January, the year eighteen forty-one. Latitude zero, longitude nine. Off the coast of the Congo. Our whaling ship is pulled into a cove for the delivery. Mrs. Breeze recovering nicely. Eliza. Seven pounds. Seven ounces. Lucky seven. We heard drums. The crew cried out 'Cannibals!' I ran on deck. Natives rowed from the shore to our ship. My dear wife cried for the life of our newborn daughter. The natives climbed on board with baskets of food and drink. I commanded the crew to hold their fire. Cannibals? They were freed American slaves, now settled in Liberia. They had seen our flag and come to trade. I showed them my daughter. The oldest freedman put a crown of red flowers on Lydie's perfect head. The crown of freedom. He looked down and said this child is destined for great things. The natives bowed down and worshipped the newborn Eliza! Liza! Ly-zie! Ly-die! Ly-die! Freedom."

LYDIE BREEZE *closes the book.*

> A while ago I was so happy with what I created here and I looked out at the horizon and saw my father's ship speeding toward land, even though there was no wind, the sails billowed. The silent ship came out of the windless sea and rode up onto the beach. The ship came up the stairs. I saw my father at the prow of the ship. "Lydie!" He threw out a length of rope. Freedom! I caught the rope! I wound it around me. I jumped!

LYDIE BREEZE *reaches out. Darkness.*

SCENE ONE

Nantucket. 1895. The interior of the desolate house on the sea out on the Madaket Road. The parlor, very sparsely furnished. Stairs lead upstairs. A front porch leads out to the beach, which surrounds the house.

Dawn.

LYDIE HICKMAN, *a fifteen-year-old girl, the daughter of* LYDIE BREEZE, *enters the parlor, carrying a lit candle and a blanket with a parcel. Her right eye is covered with a white patch held on by a length of gauze wrapped around her head. Over her nightgown,* LYDIE HICKMAN *wears a greatcoat too large for her that belonged to someone else years ago.* LYDIE *places the blanket on the table.*

LYDIE

Beaty? I'm ready.

LYDIE *pounds her palm on the table in steady rhythm.* BEATY *enters, carrying a bottle of wine and a loaf of bread. A ritual begins.*

BEATY

I came out of my room. I'd been asleep. I heard the shutters banging back and forth. No air. I woke up suffocating. And yet I heard the shutters banging in the breeze.

LYDIE

But there was no breeze.

BEATY

No air. The banging. Your mother's feet swinging up there against the bannister.

LYDIE

My mother's feet swinging up there against the bannister.

BEATY

Your father heard my scream. He came out of his room. He was drawn out of bed by my scream. He is naked. She is above him swinging. Her feet making that shutter-slamming sound. Your father sees the body. He climbs up to where your mother's neck is. He takes the rope in his mouth and bites it till it is free. Your mother's body drops. Drops to the floor.

LYDIE

There. She falls there.

BEATY

Your sister runs out of her room. She sees the body. She sees her naked father. She sees you. Excuse me, she says, I'm having a horrible dream, and goes peacefully back to sleep.

LYDIE

My father?

BEATY

Your father takes your mother's face and pushes the tongue back in her mouth. He slaps her face. Breathe. Breathe. He slaps the dead woman's face.

LYDIE *opens the blanket and takes out a noose.*

LYDIE

Bring her back to life.

BEATY

And he wrapped his legs around your mother's body to hold her upright and he kept squeezing her to get the air in. Kept squeezing her.

LYDIE

To bring her back to life.

BEATY

But he failed. He failed. And he dropped your mother's body and went out the door, down naked to the beach. He swam for a long while. I thought he would die. To join her in death. It would have restored my faith in men.

LYDIE

Don't wish my father dead.

BEATY

Does he keep your mother alive? Early morning priests say mass. And the priest eats the flesh of Christ and Christ is alive for one more day. We must keep your mother alive.

BEATY *pours wine.*

LYDIE

Keep my mother alive.

BEATY *breaks bread.*

BEATY

Hoc Est Enim Corpus. Hoc Est Enim. Say her name. Her name—her name.

LYDIE

Lydie Breeze.

BEATY

We must be very still. *Et Introibo Ad Altare Dei.*

LYDIE

Mea Culpa. Mea Culpa. Mea Maxima Culpa.

They kneel. BEATY *dips the bread in the wine and reverently holds up the bread.*

BEATY

Lydie Breeze, what is it you want me to do?

LYDIE

What is it you want me to do?

BEATY

I feel this great task you want me to do.

LYDIE

I feel this great task you want me to do.

BEATY

When I die . . .

LYDIE

When I die . . .

BEATY

When I pass over to the other side, you will meet me and you will ask, "Did you do my task?"

LYDIE

Mother. What is the It?

LYDIE & BEATY

What is the It?

BEATY

We must be very still. *Hoc est enim corpus. Hoc est enim.*

They eat the bread dipped in wine.

LYDIE

Are you here? You're in this room. Near enough to see me?

BEATY

She's here.

LYDIE

Mother?

BEATY

Oh, yes! She's here. Sure as Christ is in that early morning mass. Show your mother what I'm teaching you! Lydie Breeze! Listen!

LYDIE

Take two eggs and separate. Take four cups of sugar.

BEATY

No, dear. Six.

LYDIE

Six. Stir in currants and raisins.

BEATY

Yes. Add the flour.

LYDIE

Flour. Bake. I forgot the vanilla. I forgot the nutmeg. I forgot the salt! Mother, don't listen!

BEATY

Show your mother you know the alphabet.

LYDIE

A. B. C. D. E. F. G. H. I. J. K. L. M. N. O. P. Q. R. S. T. U. V. W. X. Y. Z.

BEATY

Lydie Breeze, I'm teaching her as you taught me. As well as I can.

LYDIE

Ma, can you heal my eye?

BEATY

Of course she can heal your eye. She can do every blessed thing. Lydie Breeze, I was a child. I was a servant. Hired to work. Hired to clean. But you made me special. You taught me as I teach her how to foretell weather from sunsets. How to circle a ring on a long strand of hair to predict an unborn baby's sex. How to tell time from sticks in sand. I used to sit and listen to you, Lydie Breeze. Instructing the men. Reading. Questioning. Aipotu. You called this place—

LYDIE

Aipotu! Utopia backwards.

BEATY

And those men betrayed you. Your father betrayed her.

LYDIE

Don't say this.

BEATY

Your father betrayed her! She only wanted greatness for them. And he's forgotten. He's forgotten her. *Hoc est enim corpus.*
(*Pause.*)
She is gone.

LYDIE

No!

BEATY *stands, now matter-of-fact.*

BEATY

She is gone. Men forget. You'll see what men are.

LYDIE

I'll never see what men are.

BEATY

Oh, they'll come into you.

LYDIE

They'll never come into me.

BEATY

Have your periods started? Wait. Wait.

LYDIE

I'm never going to have periods.

BEATY

You'll see. You'll see the blood. You'll hear your body saying, "Watch me. Watch my blood." I'm getting you ready for the blood between men and women.

BEATY *fills a basin with water.*

LYDIE

I don't have periods. My friend Irene Durban and I don't have periods. We made a pact. If anything like that happened to her, she would tell me. She would send me a code. She would send me a shredded bee.

BEATY

Shredded bee?

LYDIE

She would send me a bee with its wings pulled off. I have
received no mail all summer. It won't happen to Irene. It won't
happen to me. I am safe. I am my mother. Losing my sight is
a present from her. Dead to the world so she can come in me.

BEATY *lifts* LYDIE's *bandage and bathes* LYDIE's *eye.*

BEATY

You have not lost your sight. You had an accident.

LYDIE

I have been blinded!

BEATY

Temporary. Temporary. By the end of the week, your eye will
be healed.

BEATY *restores the bandage.*

LYDIE

A week is a very long time.

BEATY

Do you want to be a little blind beggar? I'll get you a cane and
a little tin cup. We can put you outside the front door.

She puts glasses with dark smoked lenses over LYDIE's *eyes.*

LYDIE

You're a cruel person.

BEATY

A truthful person.

LYDIE

You haven't told me one thing that's true.

BEATY

I told you about men.

LYDIE

You and your men.

BEATY

One man. Only one man. And I told you about your mother. Why did you have to be born when it was all over? Why couldn't you have known your mother in all her glory?

LYDIE

We'll keep her alive. The two of us.

BEATY

If only your eye would never heal. I could be your eyes.

LYDIE

You are.

BEATY

I could always take care of you.

LYDIE

You will. Always.

BEATY

Why do you have to change?

LYDIE

I won't. I promise you that.

BEATY

Your body will change. You'll fall in love. You'll forget about your mother.

BEATY *leaves the room.*

LYDIE

I won't. I won't change.

LYDIE *takes the noose and kneels.*

Ma? Do you want me to join you before I change? Is that the It? Ma? Ma!
   (*Silence.* LYDIE *is terrified.*)
Beaty, don't leave me alone!

LYDIE *runs out of the room after* BEATY.

SCENE TWO

Later that day.

GUSSIE HICKMAN, *22 years old, steps into the house, dressed in a very fashionable yachting costume. She looks around. She hasn't been here in a few years. The room looks even more wretched in the bright morning sun.* GUSSIE *opens the cupboard and finds a bottle of whiskey. She pours herself a good stiff drink. She takes a deep breath, and calls out: "Ooooo-ooo."*

LYDIE, *in her dark glasses, bandaged eye, wearing a bright red dress, appears at the top of the stairs.*

LYDIE

Is it Gussie?

GUSSIE

Lydie?

LYDIE

Is it my sister?

LYDIE *runs down the stairs and hurls herself into* GUSSIE's *arms.*

GUSSIE

You're all grown up.

LYDIE

I've been calling out to you for months! Gussie! Gussie! I am powerful to call you here.

GUSSIE

Lydie, what's happened to you?

LYDIE

I'm blind! I went into town. A man was following me. Boys put firecrackers in a bottle. Glass flew in my eye. I'll never see again!

GUSSIE *holds up five fingers.*

GUSSIE

Oh, poor babe! How many fingers have I got?

LYDIE

Five.

GUSSIE

I think you'll be fine. How is Pa?

LYDIE

Pa's the same.

BEATY *enters with a pile of laundry.*

GUSSIE

Hello, Beaty. You're still working here?

BEATY

Hello, Augusta.

LYDIE

Are you here forever?

GUSSIE

Forever? God help us—forever!

GUSSIE *begins to wheeze. She pulls a cigarette out of her purse.*

LYDIE

Gussie, are you all right?

GUSSIE

I know the breath is there if my frigging lungs hold out.

GUSSIE *lights the cigarette and inhales deeply.*

BEATY

I would think living in Washington D.C. working for the government would improve a lady's vocabulary.

GUSSIE

Beaty, you wouldn't know a frigging vocabulary if it upped and bit you on the ass.

LYDIE

What's that funny smell?

GUSSIE

Dr. Benson's Magic Asthma Sticks.

LYDIE

Who's Dr. Benson?

GUSSIE

A man who works miracles.

LYDIE

Can I have a puff?

LLYDIE *reaches out.* BEATY *slaps her hand back.*

BEATY

No! You can't stay here, Augusta. There's no room.

LYDIE

No room?

GUSSIE

Don't worry. I'm staying on the biggest damn yacht you ever saw. A yacht the size of the Oklahoma Territory. No, I mustn't exaggerate. But I know for a fact Mr. Hearst's yacht is one foot smaller than the entire state of Rhode Island. And that's the truth. It's got a mahogany ballroom with a grand piano. And a map of the world in different colored marble on the floor. I been on it before. Not my first time. Not my first yacht either.

BEATY

You're doing very well in Washington, D.C.

GUSSIE

Shorthand. That's the key to my life. I thank God for my short-hand and my typing. It's let me meet people like William Randolph Hearst. Couldn't you make the best song out of his name?
    (Sings in a clear soprano:)
William Randolph Hearrrsssssstttttt!

LYDIE

I don't know who that is.

GUSSIE

Don't you teach her anything, Beaty?

BEATY

We're beginning with ancient history. We haven't worked our way up to the present yet. Newspapers, Lydie. He publishes newspapers. See. I'm qualified for the present.

LYDIE

Newspapers?

GUSSIE

Not just newspapers. The most powerful newspapers in America. Mr. Hearst decides what all the folks in America should think and then they think it.

LYDIE

And you're with him?

BEATY

You're his whore?

GUSSIE

Goddamnit, Beaty. I am here with Senator Amos Mason. As his private secretary.

BEATY *is astonished.*

BEATY

Amos Mason is on this island?

GUSSIE

Yes. And tonight Amos gives his great speech all about the future of America from the pulpit of the Unitarian Church on Orange Street and Mr. Hearst will have it printed up in all his papers.

JOSHUA HICKMAN *appears at the top of the stairs, unseen. He is in his mid-fifties. He carries a towel.*

You better sit down. Tonight Amos Mason is announcing he's available for the nomination as President of the United States, and Mr. Hearst will be right in the front pew, with me taking down every word in shorthand. "America's got to be kept on a gold standard or you can kiss Western civilization goodbye."

JOSHUA *comes down the stairs.*

JOSHUA

That's not a very good imitation. Is that supposed to be Amos
Mason?

GUSSIE

Hello, Pa.

JOSHUA

Hello, Gussie.

Silence.

GUSSIE

Would you shake my hand? Could you perhaps bow from the
waist? Or blink your eyes? Pretend I'm an eye chart? Pretend
I'm the "E"?

GUSSIE *begins gasping. She relights her cigarette.*

LYDIE

Gussie!

GUSSIE

I'm fine.
          (GUSSIE *inhales deeply.*)
Fine. Doctor Benson's does it every time.

LYDIE

Five years, Pa! Don't she look beautiful?

JOSHUA

She looks—

LYDIE

Like Ma?

JOSHUA

Yes.

LYDIE

She sailed in on a yacht with Amos Mason! She's his private
secretary!

GUSSIE

Pa, they're planning a war!

JOSHUA

From the deck of a yacht? I thought you'd play cards or go fishing.

GUSSIE

Hearing those two men planning which country would be the best country for America to declare war on. France? No. England? No. Spain? *Ole!* America declares war on Spain! Now Mr. Hearst and Amos just have to get Spain to do something bad to us so we can declare war on them.

JOSHUA

Why in hell would we want to declare war on Spain?

GUSSIE

Pa, the curtain is about to go up on a new century. A war will show the world the United States of America is not playing a bit part any more.

JOSHUA

Should you be telling us all this?

GUSSIE

You're my family. I'm telling you the quality of my life. My life is so rich, Pa. I want you on that yacht. I want you coming back with me. I want you to see Amos. I want you two men to shake hands.

LYDIE

Pa, to go on a yacht!

JOSHUA

Shake hands with Amos?

GUSSIE

Let Mr. Hearst hear you talk about the past. Heroes at Gettysburg. Coming up here. A renovation of the spirits. Aipotu.

JOSHUA

Why, sure! I could wear my old Army uniform . . .

GUSSIE

Now you're thinking!

JOSHUA

Sit there and whittle on my whale tooth.

GUSSIE

Mr. Hearst adores native crafts.

LYDIE

Pa, you don't whittle.

GUSSIE

Pa, Amos would forgive you.

JOSHUA

Forgive me?

GUSSIE

Pa, you can't go on like this. You were all so happy here. Shake hands. It's a new century, damnit.

JOSHUA

Oh, I see. I see. "The Senator from Wall Street" sails back to Old Nantucket to light up a corn-cob pipe with an old scare-crow from the old, old past. "Why, look at him! Amos Mason is a man of the people. He gets my vote!" Yachts! I don't go on yachts. Your father's got some principles.

GUSSIE

Pa, cut the malarkey. Amos didn't want to come to Nantucket at all. I convinced Mister Hearst. I changed the course of a yacht.

JOSHUA

You changed the course of a yacht, Gussie. You didn't change the course of history.

JOSHUA *goes out to the sea.* GUSSIE *calls after him.*

GUSSIE

Help Amos. He got you out of prison. You owe him something.
     (JOSHUA *is gone.*)
Goddamnit. Who needs him. They took his vote away. He can't even *vote*.

LYDIE

Pa was given a pardon.

GUSSIE

Amos got him the pardon. Pa never even as much as thanked
Amos for the pardon. There's schools of fish swimming around
that pardon. Look at Pa out there . . .

LYDIE

He swims out every day till I can't see him.

GUSSIE

The water looks so cold. When I was a girl, and Amos and Pa
and Dan Grady were all here, I'd watch them all swim. Ma
would teach me history from Pa's shoulders. That bullet
wound's Gettysburg. Dan Grady. The scar on his chest:
Antietam. Amos Mason. The marks on his back. You can still
see Cold Harbor.

BEATY

Does his wife mind?

GUSSIE

Whose wife mind?

BEATY

Senator Amos Mason's wife mind. You and her husband sailing
away.

GUSSIE

How did you know he had a wife?

BEATY

Don't Senators always have wives?

GUSSIE

She's in a nursing home with leprosy.

LYDIE

Leprosy?

GUSSIE

Or something. I'm not her doctor. Amos thanks God for me.
He can't take her anywhere. She's so frigging frail her arm
might fall off if anybody ever shook it.

BEATY

No wonder you can't breathe. You're poisoned inside. Living
with a married man like a whore.

LYDIE

Don't say that. Are you a whore, Gussie? A real one?

GUSSIE

I wish I was a whore. Whores sit on pink plush all day and eat
bonbons. I work my fingers to the bone. I work in the Senator's
office from eight in the morning till midnight sometimes.

BEATY

Dressed like that, you look more like you work from midnight
till eight in the morning.

BEATY *goes.*

GUSSIE

You're damn right! I dress as good as any girl can!
      (*to* LYDIE:)
Feel my dress. Can you feel the silk?

LYDIE

I never felt silk.

GUSSIE

Well, that's English silk, goddamnit. And these are my beautiful English shoes. And these are beautiful English hairpins. I
am doing so fine!

LYDIE

You went to England?

GUSSIE

Those English make me so mad. Can you imagine! We tell
England to frig off in 1776. Not till 1894 does England finally
decide to open an embassy in Washington. They infuriate me.
But Amos says I must forgive. So Amos and I had to return the
honor and go over there.

LYDIE

Did you meet the Queen? Is everything gold?

GUSSIE

I've been in Buckingham Palace. Saw Prince Edward. The Prince of Wales. He's Queen Victoria's son. The next King. We talked.

LYDIE

You talked to the next King of Wales?

GUSSIE

England! England! Are you an idiot? We were talking back and forth. If I ever get to England, I wouldn't mind looking him up. Buckingham Palace.

LYDIE

What did you talk about?

GUSSIE

Most of our chat revolved around the theatre. When you meet people of that royal ilk, you have to have cultural things to talk about.

LYDIE

The theatre?

GUSSIE

We saw *Frankenstein*. It was worth sailing an ocean for.

LYDIE

Frankenstein?

GUSSIE

Frankenstein is this wonderful scientist who cuts up old corpses . . .

LYDIE

Right on the stage?

GUSSIE

He makes this monster who's controlled by all the dreams of the parts he's made out of. Other people's dreams. Other people's nightmares. It scares the bejesus out of you. To hear all those tight-lipped English tiaras and white ties in the audience screaming like residents of Bedlam.

LYDIE

Is he hideous? Is he ghastly?

GUSSIE

No . . . Dr. Frankenstein must've got hold of the best-looking
parts of all the corpses because the monster is . . . truly attractive. He pulls you toward him.

LYDIE

I don't want to go near him.

GUSSIE

In the last scene, the doctor goes up to the North Pole, where
he's chased the monster!

LYDIE

They have the North Pole right on stage!

GUSSIE

And they walk across the ice! And it's quiet . . . It's very still . .
        (GUSSIE *spins LYDIE around.*)
And you hear the wind swirling . . . And you know the monster
is out there somewhere . . . Woooo . . . Woooo . . . !

GUSSIE *hides.*

LYDIE

Gussie? Gussie, don't scare me!

GUSSIE *sneaks up from behind* LYDIE.

GUSSIE

And the monster leaps up . . .
        (GUSSIE *grabs* LYDIE, *who screams with pleasure.*)
And he grabs Dr. Frankenstein and pulls him down, down
under the ice.

LYDIE *and* GUSSIE *fall to the floor.*

LYDIE

No!

GUSSIE

And the monster looks out into the audience in the dark
theatre. "Come, my enemies, we have yet to wrestle for our

lives. My reign is not yet over." Every evil ugly thing that ever happened woke up inside me. Ma killing herself. Pa going to prison. I got asthma worse than ever.

LYDIE

I hate the evil ugly things inside of me.

GUSSIE

You're a goddamn little saint. You never did anything bad.

LYDIE

Ma killed herself. Maybe over something I did.

GUSSIE

You were just a baby. Ma killed herself because she was still in love with the other man.

LYDIE

Dan Grady. I know the name of Dan Grady.

GUSSIE

Pa killed Dan Grady, and Pa went to prison. And then Pa came home, and then Ma died. It was all for love. All for love.

LYDIE

Gussie, were you ever afraid of Pa?

GUSSIE

Yes, I was afraid of Pa. After he came home from jail, I could never sleep at night. If I was a bad girl, I was sure Pa would come in and kill me the same as he did to Dan Grady.

LYDIE

Is that why you left home?

GUSSIE

I dream all the time I'm going to be killed. I'd rather be killed by a stranger than have Pa be the one.

LYDIE

Don't say that about Pa.

GUSSIE

Sometimes I wish they had left Pa in that Charlestown prison.

What'd he ever do for any of us? Look at you. What's he doing
for you? You can't read.

LYDIE

I can. A bit.

GUSSIE

You get decent grades in school?

LYDIE

I don't go to school.

GUSSIE

Do you know your ABC's?

LYDIE

Beaty teaches me.

GUSSIE

Those letters you write to me.

LYDIE

They're love letters.

GUSSIE

I can't read your letters. Zulus in darkest Africa send out better love letters.

LYDIE

It's very hot in here.

GUSSIE

How're you going to learn shorthand if you don't even have any
longhand?

LYDIE

I don't want to learn shorthand.

GUSSIE

Don't you care about your life?

LYDIE

I care! I'm fine!

GUSSIE

Don't Pa care?

LYDIE

Pa cares.

GUSSIE

Some people even say Pa is not your real father. Amos Mason
says Dan Grady is your father. If he is, I envy you.

LYDIE

You never come home. You never answer my letters.

GUSSIE

Baby, maybe I have kind of ignored the family the past few
years. But I come back—see this—I think Ma'd like you traveling with me.

LYDIE

But Ma is here. I hear Ma's voice everyday.

GUSSIE

I only hear my own voice. And my own voice is saying that I
want you to learn shorthand so bad. That's the ticket. When I
went down to Washington, I just showed up at the Capitol
building. Amos could've thrown me out with a gold piece. But
he didn't. He took me in and he's taught me to read and recognize the good things.

GUSSIE *strokes* LYDIE'*s face.*

LYDIE

Your hand feels so nice.

GUSSIE

Oh, baby, I'd love you to meet Amos. You'd score a bull's eye,
Lydie. A pretty young girl in Washington. And you could keep
me company.

LYDIE

But I have to stay here with Pa . . .

GUSSIE

Pa! Pa lost Ma. Pa lost me. Pa lost Amos as a friend. Pa won't even notice you're gone. Baby, electricity's been invented. I'm introducing you to power. You got a bag? I'm packing you up and taking you away.

> LYDIE

I don't want to be like you. I don't want to go into bed with everybody.

> GUSSIE

What do you know about going into bed?

> LYDIE

Beaty tells me about going into bed.

> GUSSIE

Beaty don't know nothing! Hills of beans have flags in them announcing what Beaty knows!

GUSSIE *wheezes. She rummages through her purse to find another Dr. Benson's Magic Asthma stick. She pulls out a hankie and a small medicine bottle. She finds the cigarette. She lights up. A young man named* JUDE EMERSON, *18, enters.*

> JUDE

Hello? Miss Lydie Hickman?

> LYDIE

Who is that? I can't see you. I caught a splinter of glass and it ripped my eye.

> JUDE *(Very loud)*

Hello! I'm Jude Emerson! I'm working down the beach!

> GUSSIE

You don't have to talk so loud. She hurt her eye. She didn't go deaf.

> JUDE

I ran into Doctor Grouard in town and he asked me to drop this medicine off to you.

JUDE *holds out a small bottle.*

GUSSIE

You don't have to say it with such a big smile. You should see him, Lydie, with the biggest smile plastered on his puss.

JUDE

I get nervous around sick people.

LYDIE

I'm a very sick person.

JUDE

My parents are Christian Science and we're never allowed to talk about sickness, so when I see somebody sick, I go to town. I'm a sucker for coughs and you with your wheezes, ma'am.

GUSSIE

Well, you came to the right place.

JUDE

See, my mother and father would say this lady here had nothing wrong with her eye. That nothing really happened.

LYDIE

You send your parents right over here and they'll see if it happened or not.

GUSSIE

And bring Mary Baker Eddy, while you're at it.

JUDE

She doesn't come to Nantucket. I wish she would.

GUSSIE

A little Christian Scientist working for a doctor?

JUDE

Oh, no, ma'am. I just know him from mowing his lawn last summer.

LYDIE

Is that what you do?

JUDE

I work for the government.

LYDIE

My sister does, too. She works in Washington.

JUDE

The Federal Government? Me, too! I band birds. I set up nets and catch birds that come to feed under the net and then let the net drop and I band the birds I've caught. See how far birds have traveled.

GUSSIE

And you do that for a living?

JUDE

Oh, yes, ma'am. This week I'm here. Usually I'm over by Miacomet Beach. Or Ladies Beach.

LYDIE

I go to Ladies Beach!

JUDE

I'll be at Ladies Beach all next week.

LYDIE

I'll come look for you.

JUDE

Good!

LYDIE

If I ever get my sight back.

JUDE

You put your faith in Jesus the Physician and he'll give you your sight back.

GUSSIE

I think she better try the drops.

JOSHUA *returns from his morning swim.*

JUDE

Mr. Hickman? I saw a man on the beach, and he gave me a letter to give to you.

JUDE *hands* JOSHUA *a letter.*

GUSSIE

You're a regular Santa Claus.

JOSHUA *opens the letter.*

JUDE

He was dressed in black on such a hot day. He looked like a
raven. The man carried the letter all the way from England. I
never saw such a stamp. Queen Victoria! What a good-looking
woman.

GUSSIE

You're easy to please.
  (JOSHUA, *shaken, goes to the cupboard, takes out
  the whiskey and pours himself a heavy shot.*)
Pa, you are shaking. What was in that letter.

JOSHUA

Don't smoke those damned cigarettes in here.

JUDE

It's real exciting in town. Mr. William Randolph Hearst sailed
in on a yacht this morning with Senator Amos Mason. Sir, do
you think I could ask your daughter to come into town with me
tonight to hear Senator Amos Mason?

LYDIE

I'll be sick a real long time. I doubt if I'll ever get well.

GUSSIE

Well, take the damned medicine and you'll be cured, and I'll
see Amos and I'll be cured, and Pa will have another drink and
he'll be cured. Tell me, Jude, what do your parents say about
Senator Mason?

JUDE

They think he's a real triple donkey.

GUSSIE

And I was just starting to like you.

GUSSIE *puts* JUDE'*s medicine in her purse and goes upstairs.*

LYDIE

Pa, would you put the drops in my eyes?

JOSHUA

What drops?

JUDE

For her eyes. Doctor Grouard asked me to bring them over.

JOSHUA

Where are the damn drops?

JUDE

I don't know. I gave them to the lady.

JOSHUA

There they are––

JOSHUA *finds a bottle of drops on the table.*

JUDE

It said ten drops in the left eye.

LYDIE

Ten drops!

JOSHUA

It'll make you better. Lean back.

JUDE

He's a wonderful man, Doctor Grouard. If I wasn't Christian
Science I'd go to him for everything. I'd love to be sick.

JOSHUA

Here comes one.
     (JOSHUA *lifts up the bandage and puts the first drop
     in.* LYDIE *screams in agony.* BEATY *runs on.*)
Sit up. Medicine always hurts.

LYDIE

I can't believe it hurts so much.

JOSHUA

That's why it's medicine.

LYDIE

No, Pa. Please. No more.

BEATY

Let me do it!

JOSHUA

Step back, Beaty. Honey, this hurts me more than it does you.
Two.

JOSHUA *puts another drop in her eye.* LYDIE *screams in agony. Her arms fly out.*

JUDE

Dear God.

JOSHUA

Here's three.
     (LYDIE *screams again.*)
Don't wipe it out! Be a good girl. Think of your mother.

LYDIE

How many times a day do you have to do this?

JUDE

It said four times a day.

LYDIE

Ten drops four times a day. Oh dear God!

JOSHUA

Don't cry. You'll wash it all out.

LYDIE

It's burning right through to my brain.

JOSHUA

Don't be so dramatic.

LYDIE

Don't yell at me.

JOSHUA

Four. Five. There. See. You didn't scream. You get used to it.

LYDIE

Do it fast, pa. I'll hold on.

JUDE

Hold my hand.

JOSHUA

Six. Seven. Eight. Nine. Ten.

JOSHUA *puts in the remaining drops.* LYDIE *is shaking.* GUSSIE *comes down the stairs, searching through her purse. She holds up a small medicine bottle.*

JUDE

You're very brave.

GUSSIE

Has anyone seen my nose drops?

Pause.

BEATY

What's that you've got in your hand, Mr. Hickman?

JOSHUA

What nose drops?

JUDE *takes the bottle from* GUSSIE.

JUDE

What about this bottle? It says "Eye drops. Doctor Grouard. Lydie Hickman."

JOSHUA

Oh, Christ.

LYDIE

What's happened? What did you do?

BEATY

He put the nose drops in your eyes, Lydie.

JOSHUA

A simple mistake.

LYDIE

A simple mistake?

JUDE

Say after me. "Dear Jesus. My eyes will be better. There is nothing wrong with my eyes."

LYDIE

Pa, what did you do to me?

JOSHUA

I'll wash out your eyes.

LYDIE

I don't want you touching my eyes! You tried to kill me! Just like you killed Dan Grady. Beaty was right! I don't want to be in this house! Not with men! Not with any men!

LYDIE *runs out of the house.*

JUDE

It's a pleasure to meet you, sir, ma'am. I better . . .

JUDE *runs out after her.*

BEATY

What was in those nose drops?

GUSSIE

Nothing poison. She'll be all right. Mentholatum.
     (BEATY *goes.*)
Pa, what was in the letter?
     (JOSHUA *hands her the letter.* GUSSIE *reads:*)
"High and Mighty. You shall know I am set naked on your kingdom. Tomorrow shall I beg leave to see your kingly eyes; when I shall—first asking your pardon there unto—recount the occasion of my sudden and more strange return."

JOSHUA

I've got to go to Boston. Do you have money? Got to find a lawyer. People come out of the past, Gussie. They wait for a sunny day at high noon when the shadows vanish. When the summer people have gone. When you're feeling almost smug, not because everything's going good, but because everything's leaving you alone. And then the letter comes.

A MAN *appears on the beach. He is in his late twenties. He affects the pose of a dandy, dressed in a black suit, a ragged Byronic mien. But his pale face betrays a real anguish. His speech is markedly English. His whole manner is histrionic except that anguish, that pain—that is authentic.*

MAN *(Calling out)*

Joshua Hickman.

JOSHUA *retreats. The* MAN *comes onto the porch.* GUSSIE *goes to the door.*

GUSSIE

He's not here.

MAN

May I come in?

GUSSIE

You can't, I'm not dressed. What do you want?

MAN

Are you Lydie Breeze?

GUSSIE

No.

MAN

I want Lydie Breeze.

GUSSIE

She's not here either. Who are you?

MAN

Where did she go?

GUSSIE

Who are you?

THE MAN

I want Joshua Hickman!

The MAN *goes.*

GUSSIE

Come back, come back!
        (JOSHUA *comes out of hiding.*)
Pa? Pa? I've seen that man.

JOSHUA

Is he gone?

JOSHUA *goes up the stairs.* GUSSIE *follows.*

GUSSIE

Pa. I saw him in England this spring. Pa, he was the monster in *Frankenstein*. Pa, who is he? Pa? Why is he here?

The lights fade.

SCENE THREE

Shortly thereafter. LYDIE, *still wearing her dark glasses, lies on the sand. The* MAN *comes up the top of the dune. He sees her. He approaches her.* LYDIE *senses him.*

LYDIE

Pa? Don't touch me.

THE MAN

Are you all right?

He touches her gently.

LYDIE

My eyes burn so badly.

He takes out a flask.

THE MAN

Let me put water in your eyes.

LYDIE

No salt. No more burning.

He sits beside her.

THE MAN

No. No. The water in this flask—taste it—from the Indian Ocean. Mermaids have swum in this water. This water has flowed over sunken treasures, buried gold. This water's contained sailors who drowned. Hear dolphins comforting the sailors? It's all in this water. Taste it. Taste how sweet it is.

LYDIE *feels for the flask. She puts a few drops of water on her tongue.*

> LYDIE

Don't look at me.

> THE MAN

I won't look at you.
> (LYDIE *takes off her dark glasses, lifts her bandage,*
> *and dabs some of the water in her eyes. The pain*
> *subsides.*)

My name is Jeremiah.

> LYDIE

That's in the Bible.

> JEREMIAH

I'm not in the Bible.

> LYDIE

Don't look at me.

> JEREMIAH

I'm not looking at you. I don't see anything the way I remember it. It frightens me.

> LYDIE

Everything is changed. A storm. The ground gave way. The waves were so high we thought the whole island would go. This house is the only house out here now, and soon this land will go too. The water feels so cool. I'm still not seeing, but the pain is gone.

> JEREMIAH

Did someone do something to you?

> LYDIE

My father tried to make sure I was blind. Drops in my eyes.

> JEREMIAH

Fathers don't do that.

> LYDIE

My father did. He's an evil man.

JEREMIAH

I think you have too much of the mermaid water passing through your eyes.

LYDIE

He killed a man.

JEREMIAH

Why do you say that?

LYDIE

My father tried to make me blind because I might see him for the evil that put him in prison.

JEREMIAH

What is your name, little girl?

LYDIE

Lydie. After my mother. She was a saint.

JEREMIAH

Lydie Breeze?

LYDIE

Did you know her?

JEREMIAH

Where is she?

LYDIE

Her heels bumped against the bannister like shutters banging.

JEREMIAH

What are you saying?

LYDIE

I can't touch ropes. The way people feel about snakes? That's how I feel about ropes. Even string.

JEREMIAH

What are you saying?

LYDIE

My mother is dead. I would rather have a black widow spider making webs on my face than feel a length of rope.

JEREMIAH

She can't be dead.

LYDIE

Her own hand. Bought the rope. Tied the rope. Put her neck into the rope. I've done that. Put my head in a noose to see what it feels like.

JEREMIAH

I sailed across the ocean to find Lydie Breeze.

LYDIE

How did you know my mother?
        (JEREMIAH *does not reply.*)
I hate being a kid. They don't tell you anything. My favorite time is going to be when I'm old and withered and, say, twenty-eight, and I'll know secrets.

JEREMIAH

Turn around.

LYDIE

I have to be careful because Beaty said the children of people who kill themselves have a very good chance of following in those same footsteps.

JEREMIAH

Turn your face to me.

LYDIE

I have to be watched all the time. It's a treat today being out by myself.

JEREMIAH

Let me see your face.
        (*She turns to him. He grabs her by the throat.*)
Is this how it happened before? My hands went around the throat?

LYDIE *(Terrified)*

Please.

JEREMIAH

I've wanted to kill you, Lydie. The pain sometimes is so great. I sailed an ocean to tell you this. Maybe even to do this. Make it like before. I was not ready for you before. Lydie Breeze. I loved you. I was your friend. I loved you. I was only a child. Why did you do it?

LYDIE *(Quietly)*

Stop. Please. Stop.

JEREMIAH

My Lydie. My Lydie Breeze. It's still the same.

JEREMIAH *embraces* LYDIE.

LYDIE

Beaty!
    (JEREMIAH *pushes* LYDIE *away. She falls to the sand.*
    He runs off as BEATY *comes down the beach.*)
Beaty? Beaty! Help me! Beaty!
    (BEATY *holds* LYDIE.)
Don't touch me!

LYDIE *tries to pull herself free of* BEATY's *grasp.*

BEATY

It's Beaty. I'm here. You're safe. What's happened?

LYDIE

There was a man. He tried to kill me.

BEATY

There's no man. I'm here. You're safe.

LYDIE *(Whispering)*

He kissed me. He put his tongue between my lips. He touched me everywhere. He said he knew me.

BEATY

He didn't know you. They all say they know you.

LYDIE

You don't believe me?

BEATY

Of course I believe you. When I was a child a man came up this beach. He called my name. Beaty! He told me who he was. He came into me. Months later, things happened to me.

LYDIE

You had a baby.

BEATY

I had no baby. A little sore came on me. Like a red jewel. This man had given me a red jewel. The jewel grew in size. Another red jewel appeared. My body made fluids that were like poison. The sores moved onto my lips. My face was distorted. That man on this beach had put poison in me.

LYDIE

I hear the ocean. I hear the sand. I hear the breeze. I don't want to hear this.

BEATY

I had been that night on this beach a beautiful fish, someone who belonged to the sea, and that man, that Jonah, found a way to get inside me. Poisoned me. On this beach.

LYDIE

Am I poisoned now? That man touched me. He kissed me.

BEATY

You're not poisoned this time. But sooner or later they find you. This sand. This beach. Here. All here.

LYDIE

Who was the man? Was it my father?

BEATY

No. No. It wasn't your father.

LYDIE

Who? Who? Who is he?

BEATY

My Jonah has come back to this island. Amos Mason. Senator Amos Mason.

(BEATY *takes a sheaf of pages out of her apron
pocket.*)

I've written down everything that happened. Like a gospel.
I am going to send you on a mission. You must be brave. You
must do what I tell you. Take these pages. Protect them. Go
to the yacht. Find Mr. Hearst. Make Mr. Hearst read these
pages.

LYDIE

Mr. Hearst? But how can I do that?

BEATY

You must do it. You shall do it.

LYDIE

I'm afraid to go into town.

BEATY

I feed you. I care for you. Everyone has left you. I'll never
leave you.

LYDIE

You mustn't! Never!

BEATY

If you love me?

LYDIE

I do love you.

LYDIE *takes the pages.*

GUSSIE (*Off; calls*)

Lydie!

BEATY

If Amos is poisoned, then your sister is poisoned.

GUSSIE *appears on the beach.*

GUSSIE

Lydie, I've been looking all over for you. I'm headed back to
the yacht. The Senator and I have to go over his speech.

(LYDIE *stares at her.*)

I'm sorry none of you in your frantic schedules can find the time to join me, but perhaps the next time I sail into Nantucket—

GUSSIE *begins wheezing.*

LYDIE

Did Amos do that to you?

GUSSIE

Do what?

LYDIE

Did Amos Mason put the poison in you? Is that what makes you wheeze?

BEATY (*Whispers fiercely*)

Yes! Yes! Yes!

GUSSIE

What have you been telling her?

BEATY

The capitals of the states. Albany of New York. Springfield of Illinois. Montpelier of Vermont. Boston of Massachusetts.

GUSSIE (*to* LYDIE)

What did she tell you about Amos?

LYDIE

Gussie, let me come with you? Take me on the yacht?

GUSSIE

Honey, you'll really come?

LYDIE

Let me see your life?

GUSSIE

Baby, I've been dying to show off my life to somebody. We'll find some flowers and put them in your hair. Oh, Lydie, I don't know you very well, but looking at you now, I see remnants of

Ma's face. But Ma was like me. I'm in love with the future. The next king. The next president.

LYDIE *and* GUSSIE *go off together.*

                              BEATY

Dover of Delaware.
Trenton of New Jersey.
Richmond of Virginia.
Amos? Come to me? Please?
        (*Sings:*)
"When I was a child
And you were a child
In our kingdom by the sea . . ."

The lights fade.

                    S C E N E   F O U R

Dusk. The beach. Gunshots in the distance.

JEREMIAH *stands, lost in thought, smoking a cigarette.* JOSHUA *wanders onto the beach, in search of the hunters, a bottle in his jacket pocket. More gun shots.*

                              JOSHUA

Those hunters . . .
        (*He sees* JEREMIAH.)
You couldn't have known your father would hold his cigarette that way.
        (JEREMIAH *turns and sees* JOSHUA.)
Exhale that way.
        (JEREMIAH *throws his cigarette away.*)
Yes. Even toss it away like that. Have you seen the pictures of spermatozoa? Like fishes swimming back to some forgotten source. The news those fish carry. That you could smoke exactly like some entirely other person.
        (*More gunshots are heard.*)
Bam bam bam. You were thirteen the last time I saw you.

JEREMIAH

The day you killed my father.

JOSHUA

You've had quite the success.

JEREMIAH

I've had dreams of this day.

JOSHUA

My daughter saw you in London. She didn't know, of course, that I knew you—that we knew—that there was the family connection. Homicide should bind people together. She works for Amos Mason. Is that why you've come? To vote? Leave England to come back and vote for one of your father's friends? That's a good citizen. An actor who's a good citizen.

JEREMIAH

That's not why I came back.

JOSHUA

I saw pictures in a magazine of your flat in London. Windows sealed in blue silk. Frankenstein. Lots of dollars in old monsters.

JEREMIAH

I don't play the doctor.

JOSHUA

Ermine rugs on the floor. To give the illusion of snow.

JEREMIAH

I play the other part.

JOSHUA

A Russian sled in the center of the room instead of chairs.

JEREMIAH

People are always confusing the two.

JOSHUA

Spending your time offstage in that troika reading the Russian novelists.

JEREMIAH

Frankenstein refers to the doctor.

JOSHUA

And you're the other part.

JEREMIAH

I'm the other part.

JOSHUA

How long have you played the other part?

JEREMIAH

I've played the monster for five years now.

JOSHUA

Five years! And the Russian novelists in your spare time. It's a good thing you're here in the country. Good clean air will blow out those cobwebs.

JEREMIAH

You killed my father.

JOSHUA

Iodine's in the air. That's the secret of salt air. Not salt. But iodine. Healing. Red. I don't want you hurting my daughters. I don't know what you're up to coming here. But you're not to hurt my daughters. I've done time for what I did to your Pa. He was my closest friend. I do time every day missing him. I'm paying prices. You can hurt me. You can't hurt my daughters. Oh, hurt them. What the hell do I care . . . Gussie's a whore. She's Amos Mason's whore. Isn't that a kick? My old friend takes on my daughter. You could take my younger one. Lydie Breeze the Second. You ever play *Romeo and Juliet*? You could live that out with—No. Don't hurt them.

JEREMIAH

I'm curious as to what kind of scene you want us to play.

JOSHUA

I killed your father. Kill me. Spit on me. Beat me.

JEREMIAH

Kill you? Spit on you? Then beat you? What an odd order of events. Do you think I sailed across an ocean to hear you confess?

(Dramatic, self-mocking)

"Yes, I killed my cherished comrade twenty years ago on such a night as this! The same thunder! The same lightning! If I could only confess my heinous crime to the child I robbed of a parent. Harrrrk! The door knocks! Who could be there? Come in, stranger. The son! Is it you? The son of the man I slew? Kill me and free me from the hideous guilt that stains even my shadow lo these past twenty years. For every time I think of the murder, I hear the bells ring. The bells! The bells! Stop this cursed ringing of the bells in my ears!"

(Flat, cold)

You think that's what I want to hear?

Pause.

JOSHUA (Laughing)

Do it again! "The bells! The bells!" Dear, bizarre son of my most cherished friend, I have had many a sleepless night, but never at my worst have I heard bells. Do it again. I love it! "The bells!"

JEREMIAH

Stop! Freeze like that.

JOSHUA

Like this?

JEREMIAH

I wonder if my father stood the same way when he laughed.

JOSHUA

All wrong, sonny. I laugh like this. Bent over.

(JOSHUA poses.)

Your standard hahaha. On the other hand, your father . . . Dan Grady . . . when he got the hysterics, which was on the average of twice a day and three times on Sunday, he'd stand up and hold his sides. Almost falling over backwards. The laughs flew up out of his mouth into the sky. Bam bam bam. Feet slightly flat so there was a hint of a waddle. I'm being kind, seeing as how I killed him. There was a definite waddle. How do you laugh?

JEREMIAH

I haven't. For a long time.

JOSHUA

Frankenstein doesn't laugh? All that money you're raking in?

JEREMIAH

I'm not Frankenstein. I'm the Monster. The Monster's face is very still.

JOSHUA

A restful monster. Who could ask for more? God, you must be the envy of the actors' universe. All those actors looking for the one role to play the rest of their lives. You know Joe Jefferson? Good fella. He used to come up here. I'd hear him talking bout playing Rip Van Winkle. Fifty years now. Said anybody can play a new part every day. But the art it takes to play the same role every day of your life. Jamie O'Neill. "Count of Monte Cristo." Security. Regular income. You're a lucky man. The actor who found the role. It's what Amos Mason is preaching for America. Find the role. Find the power. The peace of the proper role. To be well cast in one's life. You should smile. I'd like to see if your father's smile landed on you. Bam bam bam.

JEREMIAH

I don't smile.

JOSHUA

Just one.

JEREMIAH

I'm embarrassed by my front tooth.

JOSHUA *lifts up* JEREMIAH's *lip.*

JOSHUA

Chipped? I think if you can afford sleds on ermine snowbanks in your parlor, you could afford to get a chipped tooth fixed in a snap.

JEREMIAH

I keep it chipped as a memento of that day. The chip keeps
snagging onto my lip. I can always taste the blood of that day.

JOSHUA

What day . . . ?

JEREMIAH

The day all the talk about Utopia and harmony finally stopped.

JOSHUA

We were still talking about that when you were a kid? God, I
thought we'd outgrown all that Utopia yakety-yak . . .

JEREMIAH

I'd lie in my bed and hear you and Amos and my father talking
about the universe being one and man willing utopias and finding new worlds in yourself.

JOSHUA

Just reliving times out of the trenches. Fancy words to munch
along with the rye whiskey. You were up there listening to
that? Poor sucker. We should've brought you down and wised
you up.

JEREMIAH

That day it all ended, you ripped the bottle of Moxie right out
of my mouth. Chipped the tooth. Do they still have Moxie?

JOSHUA

Brown. Bubbly. Bitter. The lowest. Not my idea of a treat. Yes,
they still got Moxie. I can't believe this. I'm sweating here,
drowning under my arms. This man has come back to avenge
his father's death? Is that it? Hell no! He's come back to avenge
his front tooth. I love actors. Is that what you're stewing over
in your London parlor with the Russian silk sky? Is that why
you sailed over oceans? The vengeance of a front tooth!

(JOSHUA *pulls out his bottle.*)

I can't hold back anymore. Let's have a toast to the wonder of
human vanity.

(JOSHUA *takes a swig, then offers the bottle to* JERE-
MIAH, *who turns away.* JOSHUA *leans in to him, fierce:*)

Yes! I chipped your tooth on my, repeat, *my* bottle of Moxie. The summer was ending. It was Sunday morning. Oh, I am thrilled by the depth of this confrontation. We'd finished drinking the night before. Amos. Your dad. Me. The only piss worth drinking was not worth drinking. Maybe if I cut it with Moxie? And the Moxie was gone. Oh, I love telling this story. Count Leo Tolstoy, step right up. And I spot this little sea gull dropping called Jeremiah Grady, with his thirteen-year-old lips wrapped around my cool bottle of Moxie that I had hid away because when you're bunking together in the best of Utopias you got to be careful of your own so there's no trouble, and the Sunday morning sun is making gold out of that Moxie, and I want to cut my rye whiskey with it because I'm not a pig, for Christ's sake, and I ripped that bottle out of your mouth and poured it into my rye, and I could've been a happy man today and your father alive and all of us rocking and enjoying your triumphs, but you had to start crying. The sea gull dropping has got to start bawling and spitting blood out of his mouth.

JEREMIAH

I held my tooth in my hand.

JOSHUA

Your father and I could be sitting here welcoming Amos Mason. My Lydie Breeze might still be alive. Bringing us ice to put against our faces. My two daughters happy around me. Your father alive. Me not a jailbird. A friend killer. We might all be alive. But you had to start crying. Who would have thought that Sunday morning caterwauling would end up weeping for an entire way of life. Broke up the commune. Sent Amos to Washington. Me to jail.

JEREMIAH

And me to England.

JOSHUA

Then, buddy, you should pay me a fortune for letting you play a monster sitting on blue ermine. Those spermatozoa must have swum through some mighty lavender waters. You wearing black because of Oscar Wilde? Is he one of your chums? Your father hears you bawling. He and Amos are working off their headaches, sweating out the booze tossing horseshoes. I said, that man is not going to trample me. Hey, Dan Grady, you wasn't in the cavalry. He kept walking toward me. And you're at the edge of the porch. Holding on to that face, Monster. I bet you save money on makeup. Your face wasn't going to fall off. You didn't have to hang onto it for dear life.

JEREMIAH

"Danny! Danny! He broke off my tooth."

JOSHUA

"Danny, Danny, he broke off my tooth." And that was the frigging swan song that ended how many lives? I sang right back as your father came to us, ponied up to us. I said "Your kid stole my frigging Moxie. Why do you teach people to steal other people's belongings? Your kid's got his lips wrapped around other people's belongings."

JEREMIAH

"Go buy another one." My father said that.

JOSHUA

"It's Sunday. The market's not open." Why did I sound guilty?

JEREMIAH

"Kelsey's is open."

JOSHUA

"Too far to walk. Let your frigging thief kid make the walk."

JEREMIAH

My father takes my hands off my face. He sees the missing tooth. "Did you steal the Moxie?"

JOSHUA

And you're batting those Little Lord Fauntleroy eyes. "I didn't I didn't I didn't steal the Moxie."

JEREMIAH

You said, "I think your kid's a liar."

JOSHUA

And now you segue into this frigging Oliver Twist more-por-ridge voice, "Beaty gave me the Moxie." But Beaty has oh so conveniently gone off to church. What an actor. Acting. Lying. A star liar then. And a star liar now.

JEREMIAH

And my father ran up on the porch and beat your face with that horseshoe, and all the doors opened as if floors tilted up and the ocean tilted up and people slid down onto the scene as you and my father went at it. A brown stain appears at the back of your swimming suit. Amos calls out laughing, "Dan Grady's doing it! He's beating the actual shit out of Joshua Hickman." Lydie Breeze, your wife, circles my arms. My ears. Lydie Breeze struggles me up on the porch. I fall onto my knees. I watch the fight through her legs, her thighs. I press myself against her. Smelling the sea on her body. I cool my face against the thigh of Lydie Breeze, her bathing costume wet. Seaweed like a birthmark on the hip of Lydie Breeze. Blood from my mouth trickles slowly down her leg. I taste her. I felt so safe. Two men fighting over my honor. Silver horseshoes exchanging hands. Invisible stallions in full gallop. She screams for you both to stop. Amos turns on the hose to separate you like two dogs stuck together in heat. Beaty comes home from church. "Yes, I gave the little boy the Moxie." The fight is over. Faces so bloody I cannot tell who is who. I run to the standing one. My father. I embrace him for saving me. I wipe the blood from my father's valiant face. It was you.

JOSHUA

Moxie . . . a bottle of Moxie . . .

JEREMIAH

My father. Stretched out. The women took me upstairs. Beaty brought me more Moxie, but it was too cold to drink with the broken tooth. A cart came. The horses moved slowly. No hurry, really.

JOSHUA

We had missed bullets together . . . Antietam . . . Cold Harbor . . . We had survived a war, goddamit . . .

JOSHUA *drinks.*

JEREMIAH *(Dramatically)*

"My reign is not yet over . . . Follow me to the everlasting ices

of the North. Where you will feel the misery of cold and frost
to which I am impassive. Come, my enemy. We have yet to
wrestle for our lives . . ."

JOSHUA

What the devil is that?

JEREMIAH

The Monster's big speech.

JOSHUA

That?

JEREMIAH

I perform it quite differently. I have on makeup. There's lights.
There's a spell.

JOSHUA

What do you want from me?

JEREMIAH

I've dreamed that some night, I'd see you in the audience and
step down off the stage, strangle you in your seat and step back
on the stage, and they'd all think it was part of the play.

JOSHUA

I know why you're here. You want to play Hamlet. Every actor
has a hit, he wants to start ascending Mount Hamlet.

JEREMIAH

I came to kill you.

JOSHUA

Fine.

JOSHUA *stands there openly.* JEREMIAH *falters.*

JEREMIAH

You were friends.

JOSHUA

Best of friends.

JEREMIAH

I watched my father die. The police took you away. Amos went
into town with you. The house was empty except for Lydie
Breeze and me. I heard her footsteps coming up the stairs.
Slow. Heavy. Her hair was down. She sat on the edge of my
bed. She leaned over me. She held me. She had been weeping.

JOSHUA

Bam bam bam. Where have those hunters gone . . .

JEREMIAH

Her hair fell over me like a tent. Her hair smelled . . . Oriental.
Omar Khayyam. *The Rubaiyat.* She whispered to me, "Are you
awake?" "Yes." "I loved your father." "I did too." She said, "You
fool, I loved him." And she began beating the walls and crick-
ets were in them and began squawking. She was so angry. "He
betrayed me." "How? You were all friends." "I have something
for you," she said. She reached under the sheet. Why were we
whispering? Her hair made it all so quiet. And she began
touching me. I became frightened. What was happening? "Oh
yes," she said, "you're his son. You're a man." And she rolled me
onto her and I wanted to run away because I felt a power in me
that had never existed in me before. I was thirteen. I did not
know what that feeling was . . . She pushed me aside. And then
she put her hair back and held me all shaking, and began holding me like a mother. "What have I done to you? What have I
done to you?" And she cried and she cried and she cried.

   At my father's funeral, she did not look at me. Then I was
sent to England. Before I went, it began to hurt down there
where she had taken me.

JOSHUA

Hurt?

JEREMIAH

I was afraid to tell anyone how much it hurt. I was afraid the
people in England might send me back. Put me in jail. So I
didn't tell anyone. The English relatives were so nice. The
English school was so nice. Christ! I was even disappointed in
the lack of horrors. The only horror was the pain coming out
of me. And then the doctors diagnosed me and put me on
medication of arsenic treatments, which did not poison me but

almost did. And I was told I could never have a normal life and must never touch a woman because of how infected I was, and I began to live in that tent of hair and suffocate and dream only of Lydie Breeze, who had poisoned me, and I went with whores because I had to release this need in me. And then a series of murders began in London. Brutal murders. Prostitutes. Tarts. Useless bits of humanity. Murders on streets that I had been on . . . and I became terrified and to save myself and stop the bad dreams said I will become other people who are not afraid, and I became an actor . . . and I had success . . . and now I want to face that woman and meet her as an equal. Because I am no longer afraid of her. I want myself back. I want to kill Lydie Breeze or make love to Lydie Breeze. But I come back and find she is dead. And there can be no—Revenge? I don't want that. I want her to look at me and see her poison. I don't want to play this monster. I am sick of playing this monster, and if I am asked to play it for the rest of my life I have to have a whole human being to come back to when the curtain comes down. A human being!

Silence.

JOSHUA

After Lydie Breeze died, I found a letter . . . I read it over and over . . . Trying to decipher a woman's last words. "Little man, I take you to my grave, I gave as I was given and I regret that to my dying day which is today." . . . "Little man." I made myself smaller and smaller. "I take you to my grave." I've put myself there. "I gave as I was given." I understand. The letter was for you. Her last thoughts were for you. Does that make you feel better? Does that heal wounds?

JEREMIAH *(Bitterly)*

She's forcing me to forgive her.
(JEREMIAH *puts out his hand.*)
There's no revenge.
(Pause.)
Joshua. I forgive you.

JOSHUA

Forgive me? I'm no monster who kills who he wants night after night and then turns to his audience and is applauded into innocence. Killing your father is the only true moment in my life. I keep the horror of it pressed to my skin like a hair shirt. Forgiveness! And you think you're Jack the Ripper because of what my woman did to you? A divine goddess on high passing down poison? And you'll forgive her? The arrogance! If there's anyone you have to forgive, it's your father. He picked up a dose of syph from one of his Boston whores. He didn't care. He wanted my wife. He took my wife. It's his betrayal that's ruined your life. And I ruined Lydie Breeze's life. And she ruined mine. And we all carelessly ruined each other's lives. How can you even begin to find a path to forgiveness? After Lydie Breeze died, I had them cut her open and found all this rot. I told myself— that's why she wouldn't come to my bed after I got out of prison. She was trying to protect me. How noble. How loving. I forgave her. I've stayed drunk nursing my forgiveness. And now I see what really happened. Your father destroyed her. She wanted to destroy you. And I don't fit into her death at all. No love. No love at all.

We use to read here. We used to have knowledge here. We used to dream here. America could have been great, my Jeremiah, but we never trusted our dreams. We only trust the itch in the pocket. Fuck who you want. Take what you want. We all should have been killed at Gettysburg. Caught the bullet at Cold Harbor. The War Between the States was our finest hour, us as we truly are. Forgiveness from another human being? You'll never get it. Syphilis. That's all you'll ever get from another human being. Syphilis and suicide notes.

(*Gunshots.*)

There are those hunters back again. Their bloody bags filled. I loved your father. He was my friend. He took my wife. He wasn't clean. Forgiveness?

(JOSHUA *raises his fists.*)

I could kill you all over again.

JOSHUA *advances on* JEREMIAH.

Blackout

A C T   T W O
S C E N E   O N E

Later that evening. The house. JOSHUA *comes down the stairs in a high mood. He wears his old Civil War uniform jacket, unbuttoned, and his army cap. He drinks out of his bottle.*

JOSHUA

Voices out of the past. Amos Mason! So happy to see you again
. . . That's the way I'll do it. Etiquette. "And this must be Mr.
Hearst! So happy to meet you, sir. We don't get your newspa-
per on the island, but we do get news. So, you're planning to
start a war on Spain. Good luck. Nothing like a war to bring
men together. Give a country something to do. We loved our
war. 'When lilacs last in the dooryard bloomed.' That was our
Cold Harbor blood that watered those goddamned lilacs.
Amos and Dan Grady and me. We came here after the war.
You thought Walden was a dream? Walden was a Buffalo Bill
Wild West Show compared to the austere moral splendor of
our model community. Only fitting that one of us will be the
next President of the United States. Even though Amos was
the least of us. But you'll see to that, won't you, Mr. Hearst?
You and your newspapers? You'll make Amos your creation?
Your monster? No, no, not 'monster.' 'Sponsor.' I said,
'Sponsor.' You'll sponsor Amos. Hello, Amos. You want me for
Secretary of State? To determine the policies? Define the
roles? I was head of the commune. I will consider it . . ."
   (JOSHUA *makes a toast to the skies.*)
Lydie Breeze? One of us made it. I thought it would be me . . .
   (YOUNG LYDIE, *in a panic, bolts into the house. She
   plows into* JOSHUA *and sends him reeling.*)
Goddamn you! Can't you do anything right?

LYDIE *tries to speak. She runs up the stairs.*

JOSHUA

Come back here! I am talking to you!

JUDE *enters, carrying all of* GUSSIE's *luggage.*

JUDE
Hello, Mr. Hickman. You look different.

JOSHUA
Where are you going? You can't move in here.

GUSSIE *strides behind* JUDE *into the house, furious.*

GUSSIE
Goddamnit!!

JOSHUA
Gussie!

GUSSIE
You get away from me. You stay back.

JOSHUA
I'm on my way to the yacht.

GUSSIE
If you step one foot on that yacht . . .

JUDE
Sir, I wouldn't.

GUSSIE
Why did you have to ruin my life?

JOSHUA
What did I do?

GUSSIE
Why is that your talent in life? Killing Ma. Killing Dan Grady. Is that all you do? Why would you ruin it all for me? Why would you spoil it?

JOSHUA
I haven't spoiled anything.

GUSSIE
I suppose you didn't put Lydie up to handing those pages to Mr. Hearst.

JOSHUA

What pages?

GUSSIE

What pages?
  (*To* JUDE)
You get me off this island! A canoe! A kayak! A raft!

JUDE

Sir, do you know a vessel this lady could rent?

GUSSIE

I thought you were a fisherman. You told me you were a fisherman.

JUDE (*flapping his arms*)
A bird bander. Birds. I'm a bird bander!

GUSSIE

Birds! Fish! All the same damn thing! Frigging nature! Get my English trunk out of this goddamn American weather. Everything's soaking wet and it's not even raining. Goddamn Nantucket. Damp Damp. Damp.
  (GUSSIE *opens one of the bags and pulls out silk gowns.*)
Did my perfume bottles break? I don't want perfume spilled on my dresses.
  (*She slams the case shut.* JUDE *picks up the luggage.*)
Do you have all the bags? There were three bags full! And don't you go Baaa Baaa Black Sheep to me. It's all your fault. You brought the medicine. You came on the yacht.

JOSHUA

What pages are you talking about?

JUDE

Sir, I saw on a dune this extraordinary color. Sir, it was an Oriole. A Baltimore Oriole. That bird had flown up here from Maryland. That's extraordinary. And this bird was shot down. I told the hunters to stop. They said they were guests on the yacht of William Randolph Hearst. I picked up the bird and ran into town with this dead bird in my hand, and I ran to Mr.

Hearst's yacht. Up the gangplank. I wanted to push the dead bird in Mr. Hearst's face. Guards pulled me back. Then your daughters came and . . .

GUSSIE

I'm his daughter. That's my tragedy. You might as well give me a swig of that whiskey.

JOSHUA *passes her the bottle.*

JUDE

And Lydie, as bold as a Piping Plover, handed pages to this fat man.

GUSSIE

Amos Mason is not fat.

JOSHUA

Is Amos Mason fat?

JUDE *nods yes.*

GUSSIE

The paunch of prosperity.

JUDE

Then this tall man with a high reedy voice who looked like a Diving Cormorant—

GUSSIE

Mr. William Randolph Hearst.

JUDE

Mr. Hearst says, "What's in those pages to turn you so white?" And Mr. Mason puts the pages behind his back like a guilty Magpie. "Nothing at all."

GUSSIE

Only my obituary notice.

JUDE

And Lydie says, "That man poisoned Beaty." And Mr. Hearst says, "Amos Mason poisoned who?"

JOSHUA

Lydie said what?

JUDE

Lydie said, "Amos Mason gave Beaty syphilis years ago." Now as a Christian Scientist, I don't believe in syphilis. And Mr. Hearst says, "I had best see those pages," and the fat man—

GUSSIE

Amos.

JUDE

Amos ran away, but Mr. Hearst flew very fast like a bald eagle and snatched the pages. And read them.

GUSSIE

An hour ago, I was drinking champagne on a yacht.

JUDE

And Mr. Hearst put the pages down.

GUSSIE

And now I'm swilling down rotgut in the House of Usher.

JUDE

And Mr. Hearst said, "Is this true?" And Amos said, "I never knew the woman that way." And Lydie cried out, "You did! You did!" Lydie wouldn't stop. She said to Amos. "I bet you slept with my mother. I bet that's why she killed herself." And Mr. Hearst said, "Suicide?" And Amos said, "Her mother committed suicide, but not over me. She did it over Dan Grady." And Mr. Hearst said, "Who's Dan Grady? Is Dan Grady the old friend we've come back to visit?"

GUSSIE

I said, "That was Joshua Hickman. That was my father. That was the old friend."

JUDE

"Where is Dan Grady?" Mr. Hearst has the strangest voice.

GUSSIE

And I said, "Murdered! By Joshua Hickman."

JUDE

And Mr. Hearst says, "Your father is a murderer?" And Amos says, "Sir, all this is ancient history." And Lydie says, "Not to Beaty. Read these pages. And my father may not be a murderer. He may be the victim. And he may not be my father because in the old days it was a commune and they all slept with my mother and then they murdered themselves and killed themselves and picked up disease. And poisoned each other."

GUSSIE

I think it was then I slapped her.

JOSHUA

Who did you slap?

GUSSIE

Lydie. Really hard. She had her little smoked glasses on, and they flew off her face and broke. And Mr. Hearst said, "You struck a blind child." And I said, "She's not blind."

JUDE

And then the fat man—

GUSSIE & JUDE

Amos!

JUDE

—put a curse on you, Mr. Hickman.

JOSHUA

A curse on me?

GUSSIE

On all of us. On our family. "You planned all this," he said to me. And then he called me a whore.

JUDE

And Mr. Hearst said, "Isn't she your secretary?"

GUSSIE

I said, "Mr. Mason is correct. I am his whore." *Was* his whore. I *was* on a yacht. I *was* living in our nation's capital. I *was* giv-

ing orders to yachts to change direction. From now on, it's all
was-es.

JUDE

And she also said she was pregnant.

JOSHUA

Oh, Christ! Gussie!

GUSSIE

I'm not pregnant. Don't worry. I wouldn't bring anybody into
this world. I only said that to stop Amos from throwing me off
the boat. I thought he'd be kinder if I said I was pregnant. No.
Pregnant I'm not. Homeless I am.

JUDE

And Mr. Hearst's eyes popped out, and all I could think about
was I'd like to band Mr. Hearst, I'd like to put a white government band right around his ankle. And your daughters ran off
the yacht like a flock of anxious sandpipers. And the gaggle of
servants threw the luggage overboard. And the covey of
hunters came back with their guns and bags of dead birds. And
there was Senator Amos Mason on his hands and knees with
tears in his eyes like a mourning dove. "I can explain, Mr.
Hearst. I can explain. I'll wire my wife. She'll join the party in
Newport . . ."

GUSSIE

He said that?

JUDE

And Mr. Hearst was shaking with rage.

GUSSIE

Her name is Gertrude. His wife. She's very nervous.

JUDE

I don't think Mr. Hearst will be backing Senator Mason for the
Presidency.

JOSHUA

Oh, Gussie.

GUSSIE

Stay away from me. I'm finally your daughter. I'm finally a *was*. And I'm the one who wanted to come back here. I'm the one who persuaded yachts to change course. Oh, Christ. I would sail on that yacht. And I'd lean over on calm waters, and I'd see my reflection smiling up at me out of the sea. And I'd look at Amos Mason, and I'd look at Mr. Hearst, and servants would pour wine, and men would plan wars. And no monster can climb out of this girl. The only power is the power that comes from being around power.

(*She puts on her hat.*)

I'm going back to that yacht. I'll crawl up the gangplank if I have to. "Forgive me, Senator Mason. I'm only a secretary. You thought there was something between us? Nothing, Mr. Hearst. Let me wire the Senator's wife. I'm only a secretary."

GUSSIE *runs out of the house.* JOSHUA *chases after her.*

JOSHUA

Wait a minute, Gussie! I'll come with you.

GUSSIE

Leave me alone. Stay away!

JOSHUA

Gussie! Wait a minute! Maybe I can help. Gussie!

They are gone. JUDE, *left alone in the house, looks up the stairs.*

JUDE

Lydie? Lydie?

Silence.

JUDE *leaves the house, slowly.*

SCENE TWO

Midnight. A full moon, casting shadows, makes everything phosphorescent. BEATY *sits on the beach.*

BEATY *(sings)*

When I was a child
And you were a child
In a kingdom by the sea . . .

JEREMIAH *appears.*

JEREMIAH

Beaty?
  (BEATY *does not turn to him.*)
I wanted to see you.

BEATY

I know.

JEREMIAH

You know who it is?

BEATY

Always.

JEREMIAH

I was so young.

BEATY

I knew you'd be back one day.

JEREMIAH

All roads lead back to this house. This beach. All roads lead
either to you or to Lydie Breeze.

BEATY

She's dead. Me. Only me.

JEREMIAH

Beaty. I come to you. To acknowledge my guilt.

BEATY

I've waited. Why did you do it to me? Why did you do it and then go away and leave me alone?

JEREMIAH

It was so long ago.

BEATY

No! This night. This beach.

JEREMIAH

I walked along this beach, and I saw this body shining in the water. A ghost? Breasts. Hands. Vanished. Sank back under the waves. And then I see the body again—glowing—coming out of the sea. And the eerie shine again vanished. But under the moon I could see the body stretch out on the sand. I pulled off my clothes and ran in the water. I began to glow. Phosphorous that washes in in great chunks in late summer and you see it catch on your body and live for a moment out of the sea like fireworks. And I felt the urge rise up in me that had come with Lydie Breeze, only this time I was not afraid of it. And I came out of the sea and stood over you, Beaty. "Who is that?" you said.

BEATY

Who is that? Amos? Mr. Mason?

JEREMIAH

I didn't want to be Jeremiah Grady. I said, "Yeah. Yeah. I'm Amos Mason."

BEATY

You noticed me?

JEREMIAH

Yes. Oh, yes.

BEATY

You're all so fascinated with Mrs. Lydie Breeze Hickman. She's so beautiful.

JEREMIAH

Oh, no, Beaty. Only you. I loved being someone else. I was suddenly strong and witty and a man and not afraid. This thirteen-year-old boy on this dark beach became Icarus and could fly and, by God, my wings were not wax. They were real and I flew right into that sun and did not melt and then fall. I was Amos. I was not afraid. I felt strength. I felt power.

BEATY

You are the first. The first man. The first night. Now! What's happening! I am amazed! Be careful!

JEREMIAH

And I came into you. And we washed the sweat off in the sea and we shone. We shimmered together in the late summer sea. The phosphorous clinging to us now for just moments.

BEATY

The two of us.

JEREMIAH

This night of large stars.

BEATY

This beach.

JEREMIAH

This beach. I didn't realize until later the price of that power. The poison. The syphilis. Passed on to me by a woman who was seeking revenge. And the revenge passed on to you.

BEATY

I'm not supposed to touch or be touched.

JEREMIAH

We share that.

BEATY

Never anyone but you. Nothing can be transported; things must stay where they are. I must stay here.

JEREMIAH

Beaty, I have to find some kind of forgiveness . . . To make up for the pain I know I've given you.

BEATY

I know the secrets of your body.
(BEATY *touches the back of* JEREMIAH's *neck.*)
Yes . . . Here is the scar. The small hairs. The gentle skin. I
imagined even that your wife never found that place.

JEREMIAH

Wife? Beaty, look at me.

BEATY

Today, when Gussie Hickman was playing the braggart about
you, I tried to destroy you.

JEREMIAH

Beaty, I'm not Amos. I never was Amos. I'm Jeremiah Grady.
Dan's boy. I'm an actor. I am very successful. I play a monster,
and each night I look out over that audience and I see them
admiring me, giving me their love. And I want to scream out
"Don't root for me, the mute victim of man's failure. Applaud
the person who dreamed me, who created me." You, Beaty.
Inside you I . . .

BEATY

I tried to destroy you today. Have you come here to kill me?
God, I've seen murder here. This beach. Streaked with blood.
Mr. Grady's body . . . I'm only a child. Where will I go?

JEREMIAH

Dear God . . . I've made you mad. You're here. Waiting for me.
To what end?

BEATY

To what end? This night. This beach. We are what we are for
only a few moments in our lives. My moment came loving you.
You in me. That's all I have. I'd hear all your voices when I was
a child. Dreaming of the future. I could never be part of your
future. I was a servant. But then one night you made me part
of your dream. I've walked in my sleep waiting for you to
dream me again. And you're here. I called you here.

JEREMIAH

Lightning strikes the monster. I come to life. That moment

only happened with you. This night. This beach. Never again. I came here like some avenging angel and end up begging forgiveness of the universe.

BEATY

Amos?

Pause.

JEREMIAH

Yes.

BEATY

You are Amos.

JEREMIAH

Yes.

BEATY

And you love me?

JEREMIAH

Yes.

BEATY

Hear the tide beginning to come in. We could sail a boat. Find the phosphorous.

JEREMIAH

Tip the boat over.

BEATY

Go under the sea.

JEREMIAH

Find a beacon. A great Statue of Liberty.

BEATY

Me! I'm the Statue of Liberty.

JEREMIAH

I'll swim into you.

BEATY

Swim into me.

JEREMIAH

Swim into your legs. Swim into your torso. Swim into your breasts.

BEATY

Swim into my torso. Swim into my breasts.

JEREMIAH

Swim into your throat. Your face. Your crown.

BEATY

You'll be home. Let the earth forget its dreamers. Take me to the sea. Wash away all the pain. I forgive you. Take me to the sea.

He takes her hand. The sound of the sea. They go into the dark.

SCENE THREE

YOUNG LYDIE *sleeps, fitfully, troubled, her eye still bandaged.*

A light shines in the darkness.

LYDIE BREEZE *appears holding a lantern and kneels over her sleeping daughter. She strokes* YOUNG LYDIE's *hair.* YOUNG LYDIE *reaches out.* LYDIE BREEZE *takes her daughter's hand and stands, pulling her daughter to her.*

YOUNG LYDIE *sits up, terrified, holding her blanket to her.* LYDIE BREEZE *goes into the dark.* YOUNG LYDIE *kneels.*

LYDIE

Ma? Beaty? Ma? Where are you? Beaty? Ma came for me just now. She came up the stairs to get me and I got scared. I pushed all the furniture against the door. Beaty. Beaty! Ma? When you came up the stairs last night, I was afraid because I didn't know how to talk to you. I thought I'd have to be dead for you to talk to me. Is that the It? You're lonely, and you want me to join you? You miss me? *Hoc est enim corpus. Hoc est enim.*

(Desperate.)
Ma, I can't hear you! I know how you did it. You took the rope.
You threw it over the rafter. You tied it around your neck. And
your soul flew out into the sea.

LYDIE *opens the blanket and takes out the noose, as if hypnotized.*

                              LYDIE
I'll do it, Ma. Home to you.

LYDIE *goes up the stairs.* JUDE *appears.*

                              JUDE
Lydie? Miss Hickman?
        *(*LYDIE *stops.)*
Ambrose Kenny, the fisherman with the yellow boat, went out
tonight for a run of blues, and he dropped his net and his net
caught—he was fishing and he saw a face under the water
because of the phosphorous in the water—Lydie, their hands
were bound together. Two of them. The man. And Beaty, the
girl who worked here.

                              LYDIE
Beaty . . .

                              JUDE
Ambrose Kenny recognized her. He didn't know the man.

                              LYDIE
Beaty?

                              JUDE
Their hands were tied together.

                              LYDIE
Was it murder? Is there blood?

                              JUDE
Not murder. No one said murder. Their hands. Tied with rope.

LYDIE *comes down the stairs, holding the rope.*

                              LYDIE
Rope . . . Beaty . . . Ma . . . Beaty . . . Ma . . .

JUDE

Should I tell your father? Should I wake him?

LYDIE

Don't tell anyone. Just tell me. Beaty belongs to me.

JUDE

Miss Hickman, I'm sorry to be the one to tell you. Please don't be mad at me for telling you.

LYDIE

Ma came here last night. When she couldn't get me, she took Beaty. Ma, you do want me? You want me to die like Beaty? Ma? Beaty! Beaty!

LYDIE *becomes hysterical. She starts to run out of the house.* JUDE *holds her. She falls. She struggles wildly.*

JUDE

Hey, now—Lydie!
Nobody wants you to die.
Shhh. Listen to me.
Where I work—I'd like you to see it.
I have a silk net. On four posts.
The net is silk.
I put food under the net.
I wait with a string attached to the net.
The birds fly under the net for the food and when enough birds . . .

LYDIE

Beaty holds out her hands to me!

JUDE

Lydie? Listen to me! I pull the string. The net falls. It doesn't hurt any of the birds. They're not really trapped.

LYDIE

She says, "Lydie, I miss you."

JUDE

I hold on to each bird and check if it's already been banded somewhere else, and I write down how far the bird has flown . . .

LYDIE

Beaty says, "I'm lonely. Join me. Join me."

JUDE

And if the bird has not been marked, I attach very gently a white band around its leg that says, for example—Today, September, 1895. Nantucket. We bird banders, we're everywhere.

(Pause.)

I don't want you dying, not the day I meet you.

LYDIE *is quiet.*

LYDIE

A net? A silk net?

JUDE

I'm having such good luck with birds. I thought maybe it's time to try with a person.

LYDIE *stands.*

LYDIE

Beaty. I have to see Beaty.

JUDE

They took her to Dr. Grouard's house. They need someone from the family to tell who she is.

LYDIE

If anybody has to tell them who she is, I'm the only one. Hold my hand.

JUDE

You mustn't be scared.

LYDIE

I don't think I am. No.

They go out together.

SCENE FOUR

A few hours later. The room is filled with morning light. GUSSIE *is in a silk kimono, sitting at the table, playing aimlessly with a Ouija board and reading the results.*

GUSSIE

F.O.R . . .

JOSHUA *comes down the stairs.*

JOSHUA

Where the hell is everybody?

GUSSIE

G . . . F.O.R.G . . .

JOSHUA

I got to hand it to you.

GUSSIE

You? Hand something to me?

JOSHUA

What a thrill. I have had thrills. That was a thrill. For a woman to stand up in the pulpit of the Unitarian Church?

GUSSIE

The earth did not open nor swallow me up.

JOSHUA

That took courage. Two hundred people came to hear Amos Mason and they get you.

GUSSIE *(Declaiming)*

"I have come with sad news. Senator Mason will not be here tonight as he has set sail from this treasured isle of his youth. But I thought as his secretary I would tell you what he would've said, as I wrote out the Senator's speech on my typewriting machine, so I am the next best thing."

JOSHUA

You are. You are.

GUSSIE

"America is a yacht."

JOSHUA

And then they all got up and left. Does he really say that?
"America is a yacht?"

GUSSIE

Course he don't. He says, "America is a *promise!*" But I couldn't
stop saying *yacht*. Getting back there and seeing the yacht had
sailed. Yacht. Yacht. Yacht. Did I pick up votes for him?

JOSHUA

I don't think people on an impoverished island want to hear
that America is a yacht.
(GUSSIE *reaches for another Dr. Benson's and lights
up.*)
But I was proud of you last night.

GUSSIE

Proud?

JOSHUA

You looked like the great figurehead on a ship.

GUSSIE

What kind of ship? No yachts.

JOSHUA

No, a glorious battleship. Steaming off to war.

GUSSIE

What kind of ship are you? Are you steaming alongside me?

JOSHUA

No. No. What kind of ship am I? A few years ago, a ship sailed
out of New York harbor with a hold full of treasure. A bright
jaunty crew. Sails facing the sun. Catching the breeze. Days
later that same ship was found abandoned at sea. Crew vanished. Empty. Bereft. A mystery of the sea.

GUSSIE

The *Marie-Celeste*.

JOSHUA

That was the name of the ship. Could I have a pull on that cigarette?

GUSSIE

Pa, they're not just for asthma.

She hands him her cigarette. He inhales deeply.

JOSHUA

I know that. We used to smoke these a lot up here. Dan. Amos.
Your Ma. Good old Doctor Benson. Very nice. Very nice. Not
my usual breakfast. But very nice.
    (Calls)
Beaty? Where is Beaty? Where is that damn girl? I want my
coffee!

GUSSIE

That damn girl won't dare show her face while I'm here.

JOSHUA

Make it up with her. She was your Ma's friend.

GUSSIE

I'll make it up with her. I should even give her a little present
for getting me off that yacht. Yacht. Yacht. I should stay here.
Get this house into shape. Teach Lydie to read. Get you fixed
up. You're no empty ship.

JOSHUA

What will you want from me?

GUSSIE

Oh, nothing. Attention. Sober. An education. I'd wish for san-
ity. Not to be scared. Courage. Some of that.

JOSHUA

You got all that from Amos?

GUSSIE

Amos? Amos beat me.

JOSHUA

He beat you?

GUSSIE

I thought if he beat me enough he might forgive you.

JOSHUA

Are you going back to Washington?

GUSSIE

Washington smells. All those swamps . . . I'm trying to get this damned spirit board to spell out "H.E.R.E." Stay here. But it keeps coming back to "F.O.R.G."

JOSHUA

"F.O.R.G." Forget here. Forget your father. Forget Nantucket.

GUSSIE

I beg your pardon, Pa. It's spelling out "Forge ahead." "For Gussie." "Forget me not." "Forego any bad thoughts." "For God's sake, don't despair." All "For Gussie!"

JOSHUA

I loved seeing you in that pulpit last night.

GUSSIE

Would you have voted for me?

JOSHUA

You know . . . I would've.

GUSSIE

"F.O.R.G." Oh, Pa, I'm glad to be home.

JOSHUA

Dream, dream. Doctor Benson, I must develop asthma.

MAN'S VOICE *(Offstage)*

Mr. Hickman!

A nattily dressed, but very awkward man appears on the porch. His name is LUCIAN ROCK, *40s.* GUSSIE *ducks out of the room and up the stairs.*

LUCIAN

Mr. Hickman?

JOSHUA *goes to the door.* LUCIAN *enters. He is terrified.*

JOSHUA

Yes?

LUCIAN

I have to come this early as I'm leaving later this afternoon. May I come in?

JOSHUA

You've already done that.

LUCIAN

Now how can I put this?

JOSHUA

I don't do business with people who lack a name.

LUCIAN

I am nervous. My palms are ice. My knees are gelatin.

JOSHUA

Your palms are ice. Your knees are gelatin. I'm glad each of them has a little name. Now what's your name?

LUCIAN

Lucian Rock.

LUCIAN *offers* JOSHUA *his card.*

JOSHUA *(Reads:)*
"Lucian Rock. Inventor." Oh! You're the inventor! Here for the summer. I read about you in the newspaper.

LUCIAN

Yes, I'm the inventor. A high-speed version of the sewing machine adapted for industrial use. May I sit down? The other day—my breath—Excuse me—The other day I saw a beautiful young girl in town.

GUSSIE *partially opens the door at the top of the stairs and listens.*

How extraordinary to see Aphrodite window-shopping in a summer resort. I followed her down a dark corridor. I felt her soul was calling to my soul.

Please, my flights of poetry are indicative of my interior emotional state.

I felt I had entered a dark temple for I saw scores of tiny silver lights glowing. The giggling I heard made me realize it was merely street toughs holding fireflies captive in milk bottles. A match was struck, a fuse was lit, dropped into the milk bottle. An explosion. The children shrieked. Shattered glass. This stellar member of the distaff sex reached her hand to her eyes. And this Dido, this Persephone ran out the dark back door into the bright light of mythology.

GUSSIE *closes the door quietly.*

But I refuse to let her exist in antiquities of my heart—

I've been practicing these words so I have to go at this pace.

I'm going off to Europe, sailing to England tomorrow at midnight. My high speed sewing machines adapted for industrial use are being presented at various major courts of those aforesaid countries. And I would like on my arm—

I didn't practice this part well enough. I have been in my laboratories in Schenectady, New York—On my arm the most beautiful young creature, as I said, a Persephone.

I inquired of various personages in town. Ahhh, the Hickman girl, Doctor Grouard said.

JOSHUA
This is the God-damndest thing I . . .

LUCIAN
Now wait, I'm not asking you to hand your daughter over to me today.

I will marry your daughter *tomorrow*.

I will make all financial arrangements. We will be married in Boston.

We will sail to Europe, where she'll be meeting Princes of Wales and Princesses of France.

And of course the Hapsburgs and all those Balkans.

Up into Saint Petersburg.

I know I'm an early caller and your daughter must be upstairs sleeping. I'll walk down to the beach.

Tramp along the sea. Expand my lungs. Prepare my farewell to America.

Prepare myself for your daughter's answer.

LUCIAN *starts to go.* GUSSIE *opens the door at the top of the stairs, dressed in the height of fashion, like Sargent's painting of Mrs. Phelps Stokes. She is radiant, except she has a bandage over one eye. She comes down the stairs.*

GUSSIE

Daddy, I'll be out cycling, but not into town. I've learned my lesson from fireflies exploding in milk bottles.

LUCIAN

This is the daughter?

GUSSIE *sees* LUCIAN *and stops, shocked.*

GUSSIE

Pardon me, but did I see you in the street in town the other day? I saw an Adonis meandering along Main Street, and I ran into a dark corridor to regain my senses. There was an explosion. I was not surprised, because the explosion mirrored what I felt in my heart.

JOSHUA

Gussie.

LUCIAN

Gussie?

GUSSIE

Augusta.

LUCIAN

Augusta? Is that your name? I hope I didn't frighten you. I heard the explosion. I heard you cry out. But I couldn't find you. I went to Dr. Grouard. He wouldn't tell me—the Hippocratic Oath and all. But he went to Philips Academy. I went to Philips Academy. He went to Harvard. I went to Harvard. He's a Freemason. I'm a Freemason. We exchanged the secret handshake. He broke his Hippocratic Oath and revealed to me that he had treated the Hickman girl out on the Madaket Road.

GUSSIE *pulls the bandage off her eye.*

GUSSIE

I'm fine now.

LUCIAN

Yes, it's you! By God, it's you! Augusta! Augusta!

JOSHUA

Augusta, Mr. Rock is going to Europe.

GUSSIE

Haven't I always wanted to travel! Someday! Someday! Do send postal cards. I do love to dream.

LUCIAN

I'd like to talk to you . . .

GUSSIE

Would you just wait outside, Mr. Rock? I have to fix my father's tie.

LUCIAN, *beaming happily, goes out of the house.*

You'll never tell him.

JOSHUA

How can you do this? Amos just set sail. You're going to run off with this inventor?

GUSSIE

I'll take care of Lydie. I'll take care of you.

JOSHUA

I don't need any help.

GUSSIE

Then God knows when I'll see you again.
Pa? I love you. Pa, I'm starting from scratch. Lucian Rock might hear me wheeze, but he'll never hear me cry. It's almost 1900. I'm American, by God. It's about to be my century.
        (GUSSIE *goes outside and joins* LUCIAN.)
Mr. Rock, may I ask you a very personal question? Be honest. What do you think about Universal Harmonies?

LUCIAN *sighs happily. He takes her arm. They go.*

JOSHUA

What about your clothes? What about your luggage? The
future . . .

JOSHUA *watches them leave. He looks around the desolate house for a*
drink. He opens the cupboard and reaches into it. He takes out an old box.
He opens it. He takes out a book. He sits at the table and opens it.

JOSHUA

Bulfinch's Mythology. The World and Its Origins . . .

LYDIE BREEZE, *young, radiant, appears out of the dark in her nurse's*
uniform. She is followed by DAN GRADY *and* AMOS MASON *in their ragged*
uniforms. It's them as they were in 1865. They are exhausted and radiant
with hope. They sit around JOSHUA *and look out at the sea with awe.*

LYDIE BREEZE

We are home.

DAN

Home.

AMOS

Home.

JOSHUA

Home.

LYDIE BREEZE

This is out future.

DAN

Our future.

AMOS

Our future.

JOSHUA

Our future.

LYDIE BREEZE

Together we're a great soul, capable of doing extraordinary
things.

JOSHUA
The word made flesh.

AMOS
That's the Bible.

JOSHUA
The manual of the Capitalist God.

LYDIE BREEZE
Never stopped one war.

DAN
Caused a lot. It's the past. Demolish the past.

AMOS
Isn't the Bible supposed to be a good book?

LYDIE BREEZE
No one disputes you, Amos. The Bible is a lovely book. It just
happens to be written in the wrong order.

AMOS
I don't understand.

LYDIE BREEZE
In reality, it's meant to open with the Apocalypse. The
Revelations of a world gone mad. And Jesus taken out of his
tomb and put on the cross, where he comes to life saying . . .

JOSHUA
"Father, why has thou forsaken me?"

LYDIE BREEZE
Then he comes down off his cross and performs miracles and
is soon a little boy . . .

JOSHUA
And then it's Bethlehem . . .

LYDIE BREEZE
And he's born . . .

JOSHUA
And people dream of a Messiah . . .

LYDIE BREEZE

And not till *then* does the Old Testament start . . .

DAN

With all the begats and begots and David and Solomon . . .

AMOS

And floods and Noah?

JOSHUA

And Cain . . .

DAN

And Abel . . .

JOSHUA

The cast gets smaller and smaller . . .

LYDIE BREEZE

Till it's only Eve . . .

DAN

And a few Adams . . .

LYDIE BREEZE

And they leave a fallen place . . .

JOSHUA

And enter the Garden of Eden . . .

LYDIE BREEZE

Free of all sin . . .

AMOS

The apple?

DAN

Eating apples!

JOSHUA

And they have all the knowledge . . .

LYDIE BREEZE

And Eve sees there's no more reason for her to be, and she uncreates herself . . .

JOSHUA

And Adam agrees and the garden's gone . . .

LYDIE BREEZE

And God uncreates the moon . . .

JOSHUA

Uncreates the sun . . .

DAN

And the oceans . . .

LYDIE BREEZE

The earth and the skies . . .

DAN

The light and the dark . . .

LYDIE BREEZE

Until there is only God . . .

JOSHUA

And God uncreates himself . . .

DAN

And there is only serenity . . .

LYDIE BREEZE

And the world is back where it was meant to be. Hush.

JOSHUA

Quiet.

LYDIE BREEZE

The Bible's such a lovely book. Gutenberg just printed it in the
wrong order.

AMOS

King James?

LYDIE BREEZE

Backwards. Backwards.

AMOS

Is all this true?

LYDIE BREEZE

All true.

JOSHUA

All true.

YOUNG LYDIE *enters, interrupting* JOSHUA'*s reverie.*

LYDIE BREEZE

Pa, what will happen now?

LYDIE BREEZE, DAN, *and* AMOS *move to various places in the room and sit, looking out, their faces on the future.*

JOSHUA

There'll be the service tomorrow. Beaty and Jeremiah will be buried beside your mother. We got anything to cut this whiskey with?

LYDIE

Moxie's always good.

JOSHUA

No Moxie. We've had enough Moxie.

LYDIE

Pa, there's so many ghosts here. Couldn't we leave this place? Move into town?

JOSHUA

No. Ghosts follow you anywhere. We'll stay here until the ghosts leave us alone . . . And if we're lucky, they'll dissolve into memories . . .

JUDE *enters, with a package.*

JUDE

The Doctor gave me the drops. Oh, hello, Mr. Hickman. The right drops.

JOSHUA

You put them in.

JUDE
I'm not allowed. Mary Baker Eddy . . .

JOSHUA *takes the drops. He is tense.*

JOSHUA
Lean back.

He gingerly puts a drop in LYDIE's *eye. She smiles.* JOSHUA *relaxes.* JUDE
stares down in amazement as JOSHUA *puts in the remainder of the drops.*

JUDE *(Impressed)*
Ahhhhh . . . medicine.
Mr. Hickman, I'd like to ask your permission to be around a lot
this winter.

JOSHUA
What are you asking me for?

JUDE
You're her father.

JOSHUA
Oh, yes. I'm her father.

JUDE
You'll be here this winter? Yes?

JOSHUA
We'll be here all winter.

JUDE
I'll be at Ladies Beach. No migrating for me. I'll be back
tomorrow.

JUDE *goes.* LYDIE *runs to the door to watch him go. Then:*

LYDIE
Pa, can I have the priest say an early morning mass for Beaty?

JOSHUA
If you like.
    (Pause.)
The postman left a letter for you.

LYDIE

I've never had a letter.
(*He hands it to her.*)
Pa, I'm afraid to open it.

JOSHUA

Do you want me to open it?

LYDIE

No!

JOSHUA

You mustn't be afraid.

LYDIE

Pa, how do I stop—being afraid?

JOSHUA

You make yourself smart. And you dream. You don't let it destroy you. You . . . Don't listen to me! Look at this world. Look at this life. Aipotu. Utopia backwards. Some legacy. We're all that's left.

LYDIE

Gussie?

JOSHUA

If Gussie's the legacy, God help us.

LYDIE

Pa, I don't know anything about you.

JOSHUA

I was a man who ached for a utopia.
(LYDIE *opens the letter.*)
Do you want me to read your letter for you?

LYDIE

Nothing to read. It's from my friend, Irene Durban. It's a bee. A shredded bee.

She shows him the contents of the letter. He grimaces.

JOSHUA
What does that mean?

LYDIE
A secret code . . .

JOSHUA
A shredded bee?

LYDIE
Pa, teach me.

JOSHUA *reaches in his foot locker, takes out another book.*

JOSHUA
The first night your mother brought me to this island, she had a book in her pocket. Walt Whitman. We rode over on the ferry. Starting a new life. She read to me. Just to me. Not to the others. Not to Dan. Not to Amos. Only to me. We sailed over the sea. I was not afraid.
(He reads.)
"On the beach at night alone . . . A vast similitude interlocks all. All spheres, grown, ungrown, small, large, suns, moons, planets. All distances of time."
Here, you try it, daughter.

LYDIE
(Reads with difficulty.)
"On. The. Beach . . ."
(JOSHUA nods encouragement. She smiles.)
"At. Night . . . alone."

The lights fade into dark around all of them.

Curtain